GW00630711

Freedom Entrepreneur

Why hard work causes business failure, and what to do about it

Peter Carey

Copyright © Peter Carey 2016

ISBN: 978-0-9956503-0-5

The moral right of Peter Carey to be identified as the author of this work has
been asserted by him in accordance with the Copyright, Designs and Patents
Act, 1988.

All rights reserved. No part of this publication may be reproduced,
stored in a retrieval system, or transmitted in any form or by any means,
electronic, photocopying, recording or otherwise, without the prior
permission of the author.

This book is sold subject to the condition that is shall not, by way of trade or
otherwise, be lent, re-sold, hired out, or otherwise disposed of or circulated
without the prior consent of the author in any form of binding or cover other
than that in which it is published and without a similar condition, including this
condition, being imposed on the subsequent purchaser.

Typeset by Phoenix Photosetting

Published by Cartel Books

For my mother,
who never sought to
constrain my imagination

*Twenty-five percent of author royalties
are donated to Save the Elephants,
for their work in preventing
poachers' machine gun attacks*

Contents

Acknowledgements

Writing a book is a team sport. I am enormously grateful to all the wonderful people who have offered me encouragement and support. Thanks especially to my wife Bertha, herself an entrepreneur, for her invaluable suggestions and comments. Thanks to Sarah and Brendan Engen, Paula Thomas, Mark Rhodes, Rachel Reese, Rezzan Huseyin, Mark Dhamma, Vena Ramphal and Arvind Devalia. Thanks also to Nick Williams, who continually and tirelessly found new and subtle ways to provide inspiration during the writing journey.

Thanks to the various mentees with whom I have had the great fortune to discuss business issues. They have taught me far more than I have taught them.

My thanks to all the café owners whose enticing premises and fabulous espresso kept me going for much of the writing process. Of special note, due to the sheer quantity of time that their table space was engaged: Esca in Clapham; Café Vergnano (1882) in Nice; Café Lelo in New York; Pain Quotidian in West Hollywood; and Café des Amies in Maui. You all run fabulous businesses!

Finally, special thanks to all staff members (past, present and future) of PDP, including Cindy Burnes, Betina Balle, Stephanie Drewer, James Anderson, Fay Garrett, Inma Berrocal, David Holland and Marie-Anne Denicolo. They have afforded me the invaluable luxury of personal freedom, without which this book would not have been written.

Introduction

This book is about freedom.

Freedom is not a word that's usually associated with the life of an entrepreneur. Instead we perceive the business creator's working day to consist of hard work, long hours, obsession and stress.

It can be very different.

In my view, freedom is not only possible for entrepreneurs, it is essential to being an effective business creator. How can you make appropriate decisions if you are stressed out? How can you expect to have spontaneous ideas about business opportunities if you are constantly frantic? How can you contemplate delegating your responsibilities if you are too busy to consider it? How can you be an effective business person if you are on the verge of burnout?

I have experienced burnout. It's not recommended. But, I wouldn't go back to my life before burnout for all the iPads in China. Burnout was my teacher – it forced me to stop.

In the weeks before my burnout I was doing almost everything in the business myself – taking calls, responding to emails, booking trains and planes, producing invoices, sticking stamps on envelopes, carrying sacks to the Post Office and producing the product.

I was working almost all waking hours. My laptop sat expectantly beside me on the sofa while I ate dinner. I pounded the keyboard of that faithful machine on even the shortest public transport trips. I was petrified that my failure to respond immediately to an incoming email would lead to the loss of a vital opportunity. I was juggling multiple tasks all day long, every day. There was no such thing as weekends. My non-work life was non-existent.

By a standard that seemed appropriate to me at that time, my business was doing fairly well. Since I had set up the business, four years previously, it had grown consistently in each quarter. It was exciting to see the fruits of my labours. Providing a service which customers actually wanted was immensely gratifying, and so was making money. But, with the passing of each month, I was clocking up more and more working hours. Soon there were no more hours available.

I had no comprehension of how ridiculous my life looked, and of the imminent danger that lay just ahead – danger to health, both mental and physical.

One day I awoke to find myself a wreck. I was pale and drawn, as well as malnourished and excessively sleep deprived. I knew that physically I couldn't do even one more tiny work task. The mere sight of my laptop, let alone the thought of starting it up, made me feel nauseous. I couldn't go near my mobile phone without hastening panic. I couldn't contemplate reading, less yet responding to, an email without severe anxiety rendering me paralysed. My breathing was shallow and fast. My body was so stressed that it was vibrating.

I now know that I had gone into burnout. But, at the time, I had no idea what was going on. All I did know was that I had to get away. Away from the chaos. Away from the compulsion to attend to every last detail. Away from feeling that every occurrence was an emergency. Away from doing it all, in every waking moment.

And so I escaped. For several weeks. I left the country and commenced silent retreat. Away from everything. No laptop. No phone. No people.

The break from excessive and compulsive working afforded me invaluable time for contemplation. Several weeks of doing virtually nothing gave me an opportunity to decompress, to see things in a truer light, to achieve a long-forgotten feeling of sanity, to become mindful of what is actually important. After three months, a serene peacefulness had begun to permeate my being.

Burnout, and the calmness that eventually followed, taught me that if I was to continue life as an entrepreneur, I would have to do it entirely differently. I would need to go back to the start and restructure the business. The way that the business would work in the future would need to be nothing like it was before. Everything would have to change. My own role would have to morph from being the worker to being the leader and delegator. Most importantly, in the new entrepreneurial model, I would need to spend significant amounts of time away from the business, doing non-work things and being more present.

The miraculous and surprising effect of making the changes described in this book was that my business grew faster than before. Much faster. As I worked less and less, the business grew more and more quickly. This afforded me time, not only to indulge in non-work pursuits but also to start and grow other new businesses.

Today, my life looks very different. It is calm, balanced and well-nourished. My businesses employ many people. I travel extensively, and I work when I choose to (less than one day per week on average). Burnout taught me that freedom is an essential part of being an entrepreneur.

This book is about the changes that I made following burnout. You, too, can make these changes in order to prevent yourself from ever experiencing burnout. Or, if this book finds its way to you while you are in burnout, my hope is that its pages will be your guide out of the confusion and fear, into freedom and effortlessly effective entrepreneurship.

For as entrepreneurs, we are warriors. We create, for ourselves and others, opportunities that would otherwise be forever hidden. We forge new environments by saying how things will be. We produce new products and services where otherwise they would never have existed. We change the world.

But the entrepreneur's life of self-imposed exile is a challenging one. To embark upon it takes courage. I take my hat off to you. Because you have already started. Most likely you have given up a career. You have stepped off the standard conveyor belt of life and ventured into the unfamiliar.

If you had the time to consider your achievements to date, you would congratulate yourself. Such congratulation is richly deserved.

And yet things have become difficult. Although you may acknowledge that your business is doing well, you feel under deluge – exhausted, confused and lost.

Now the greatest challenge is upon you. Will you give up on your dreams and return to your earlier life? Or will you move forward as the *freedom entrepreneur*, creating ever more growth opportunities for your business and freedom for yourself?

This book is about why hard work is probably your single greatest enemy on the road to business success, why the work that you are currently doing is almost certainly the wrong type of work, and how to go about making the changes that will produce freedom for you and effortless success for your business.

Prologue – a familiar story?

Eighteen months after starting her business, Sally felt that she had left her life as an employee far behind.

She was now making some money from serving her customers. Not as much money as if she had remained in her old job, but it was money that she had made herself, all on her own. She was vindicated. She could honestly call herself an entrepreneur.

The people in Sally's life were now treating her differently. Those that had previously done their best to persuade her against leaving her job had changed tack. They were starting to enquire how she was doing. Some of them were even curious about how she had managed to achieve so much since leaving her employment.

At her core, when she allowed herself the time to think about it, Sally was delighted with what she had created. She was indeed an entrepreneur. She had escaped the world of working for someone else. She had become self-determined. She now knew that she could never go back to a regular job. She had achieved what many people dream about, but few actually accomplish.

But her world was not without challenge.

Although she didn't mention it to anyone, she was exhausted. True, she had some good customers now, and the income level was continuing to rise, but she hadn't anticipated that she would be working for so much of the time.

Sally was now putting in far more hours than she had worked as an employee. In many ways that was fine, as she was building her business. She didn't resent the work as such. But she was now working every evening, as well as all day.

She thought about her business all of the time. She couldn't wait to finish each meal so that she could get back to checking email and handling issues that needed to be dealt with. She woke in the middle of the night to find her brain working on solutions to challenges that her business faced.

Sally had virtually no social life now. That was fine because she was building her business. But she did miss her friends, at least when she allowed herself the time to think about it.

There was an unnerving semi-evolved thought at the back of her mind that something was not quite right. It seemed that the way that she was doing things wasn't sufficiently productive, but she couldn't seem to figure out why. She felt as if some choices that she had made were unsatisfactory, but she couldn't determine which ones they were, or what choices would have been better.

Sally would love to hand over some of the important bits of the work to someone else, but she felt certain that she was the only person who could really do the job properly. She would love to employ someone to handle the administrative aspects of the business, but how would she find the time to train someone else on how the business operates, let alone to manage them and check their work? And how would she afford to pay them?

She occasionally thought back to the time when she was an employee. Although she had always felt that she didn't want to work for someone else, at least she had good holidays back then. She dreamed of taking some time out to sit on a beach, but she knew that was impossible. Not right now. Not while she was building her business.

Sally remembered that before she had started on the entrepreneurial path, she had a vision of what that life would be like. There would be wealth and freedom. There would be admiration from others. There would be time to do all the things she had wanted for so long to do. She would be content. She would be relaxed. And she would be fulfilled.

She knew that those things lay ahead of her. But right now they seemed far off. She just had so much work to do, queries to handle, emails to send, orders to administer and strategies to organise.

Things would of course get better as the business grew, as she got more customers, and as she made more money. That was the bright future that awaited her. To hasten that day, she would work even harder. She would push the thoughts of free time and partying to one side. Things would definitely get better. But right now she was building her business.

Part One

Why Hard Work Doesn't Work

"By letting go it all gets done.
The world is won by those who let go,
but when you try and try,
the world is beyond winning."

– LAO TZU

What hard work is (and why you must avoid it)

This book is not about hard work. It's about the opposite.

But before we can consider what the opposite is, and how we can access it, we need to know what hard work is, why entrepreneurs feel so compelled to do it, and why it is so very dangerous to the success of a business to engage in it.

I did hard work because I was terrified of failure, because I didn't imagine there could be any realistic alternative, and because hard work became an addiction. I believed, simply because I didn't know any better, that hard work was a necessary part of creating a successful business.

Of course, there is nothing wrong with hard work. The problem is that as time goes on, the behaviour of hard work becomes self-reinforcing. The more you do it, the more it becomes necessary to do it, and the more challenging it is to change things for the better.

What is hard work?

For the purposes of this book, hard work has two aspects.

The first aspect is the *quantity* of work that you are doing. Hard work is excessive quantities of work. Most entrepreneurs become obsessive in the amount of work that they do. Working within the business takes up the vast majority of their non-sleep time. On a scale of priorities, hard-working entrepreneurs tend to regard the activity of working as more important than everything except eating and breathing (and, sometimes, they even forget to eat). If they had the time to think about it, they would surely realise that the hard work they are doing is not sustainable – that it will eventually result in poor health, loss of friends and burnout.

The second aspect is the *type* of work. Most entrepreneurs do the wrong type of work. The wrong type of work is actually very hard work indeed. If you are a frantically busy entrepreneur, especially if you are working alone, it's likely that almost everything you are doing is the wrong type of work. This book describes the type of work that it is appropriate for you to do in order to achieve rapid business growth and personal freedom.

Hard work, both in terms of quantity and type, has the opposite effect to that which most people anticipate. Rather than lead to certain success, it makes business failure much more likely. This is because the best qualities of the entrepreneur are obscured by hard work.

Hard work stymied the success of my business because it prevented me from being effective. Hard work, though irresistible to me at the time, was in fact my worst enemy. Hard work eventually led to personal breakdown.

Why do entrepreneurs do hard work?

I believe that we do hard work because we feel that we have to. We believe that the fulfilment of our aspirations will result *only* from hard work.

We are informed, almost everywhere we look, that hard work is essential to business success. Well-known entrepreneurs tell us, in television shows and in books, that "it takes hard work to succeed". Our parents probably taught us that we must work hard to achieve our goals. And our schooling, both in childhood and as young adults, programmed our minds with similar messages.

So we come to believe that other people's success has been achieved through considerable, perhaps even superhuman, effort. That is not an unreasonable belief. After all, the scientific principle of 'cause-and-effect' is well known. But is it true for the entrepreneur herself? Are we sure that the relevant cause (the amount of work that you do) is proportionate to the desired effect (the success of your business)? Could there be other factors to consider?

The way of the freedom entrepreneur

Some business creators openly say that, although hard work was at one time a distinct feature of their lives, it no longer is. While the creation of their first business involved hard work, they have learned that hard work was actually not necessary.

For the new businesses that they now create, these entrepreneurs don't work very hard at all. In fact, their lives are now more about other things, such as travelling, playing golf, reading books, watching sports, sailing boats, learning languages, practising yoga or attempting to beat world records. In essence, they have migrated from being hard-working entrepreneurs to being freedom entrepreneurs.

There is one important difference between the life of a hard-working entrepreneur and the life of a freedom entrepreneur. A freedom entrepreneur's life has its foundation in freedom.

The *freedom entrepreneur* deliberately builds large quantities of non-work time into every day. The freedom entrepreneur knows that non-work time is vital for producing the mindset that is necessary for freedom entrepreneurship. In other words, the inclusion of significant amounts of non-work time into your day, every day, is crucial for the success of your business. Without it, your business is at great risk.

And so we are presented with an intriguing conundrum. How do we grow our business more quickly, and at the same time work less? The answer is presented in this book. It starts with making a change in our *thinking*.

The problem for most of us is that we were not trained to think like entrepreneurs. We were trained to think like employees. Rightly or wrongly, this is what the education system prepares us for.

For an employee, doing hard work is necessary to progress within an organisation. Hard work results in the employee getting noticed. Bosses are impressed, and a pay rise and better job title follow. Since hard work is rewarded, the behaviour is reinforced. Even more hard work follows, leading to higher income and greater promotion. And so it goes.

As an entrepreneur, on the other hand, there is no one to impress but ourselves. We don't have a boss to award us a promotion or a bonus. Hard work is actually not appropriate in this new environment because it's based on a false assumption. The false assumption is that hard work is the one and only route to success. What we must do, if we are to escape from the hard work paradigm, is to think less like an employee and think more like the freedom entrepreneur. In order to do this, our focus must switch from hard work to personal freedom.

To put it in basic visual terms, let's say that the left side of the diagram below shows the time split between work and non-work activities for an average day in the life of the hard working entrepreneur, Entrepreneur A. This entrepreneur works almost all of his awake time. This kind of time usage may be familiar to you. It may even look like your own working day.

Now take a look at Entrepreneur B. For this person, work is secondary to the other activities of the day. Entrepreneur B is the freedom entrepreneur.

The goal of this book is for radical change, so that the composition of your day more resembles the right hand side of the diagram, the day of the freedom entrepreneur.

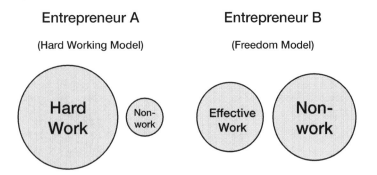

This book is about transforming your entrepreneurial life from excessive working practices into freedom-based effectiveness. We will do this in steps. Each step is a necessary part of the journey.

Part One looks at why hard work on the part of the business creator is not only counterproductive, but is actually likely to result in business failure. It is important to fully understand the reasons why hard work causes businesses to fail, so that you can begin to comfortably accept the alternative.

Part Two looks at how to change your thinking so that you start to think as the freedom entrepreneur. A change in thinking is needed because thinking is the foundation of action – assuming that you are currently doing hard work, you will need to take very different action from now on.

Part Three describes the steps that are needed to begin to set aside hard work. It includes exercises that prepare you and your business for your transformation into freedom-based entrepreneurialism.

Part Four looks at when and why you need to involve other people in your business, what type of people they will be, and how to go about setting up the necessary relationships.

Part Five explains why you are currently doing the wrong type of work, and how to achieve rapid business growth by doing much less and doing it radically differently.

Part Six looks at who and how you are being. Freedom entrepreneurs have a 'way of being' that is different from hard working entrepreneurs.

Let's get started by looking at why hard work is entirely counterproductive to your goals.

Hard work obscures the Big Picture

As busy entrepreneurs, we are often so involved in the details of the day-to-day hard slog that we have no time to see what is actually going on.

The Big Picture, a clear and unobscured view of which is indispensable for the freedom entrepreneur, is hidden by the busyness. This is unfortunate, because having access to the Big Picture is vital for business success.

What is the Big Picture?

The Big Picture is the overview, the helicopter view, the detached view, the unemotional view. It's what you see when you strip away all the extraneous information. It's the bare bones of your business, stark and clear. It is also your own fundamental aspirations for your business, in other words the reasons that you became an entrepreneur. The Big Picture must be your constant companion.

Without the Big Picture, you do not have access to two invaluable pieces of data: you cannot see *where you are* in the present moment, and you cannot see *where you are going*.

Why is it necessary to see where you are, and where you are going?

Imagine being blindfolded and taken, by helicopter, to a jungle covered area of a large Caribbean island. Your blindfold is removed and you are instructed to walk to the island's main town. The helicopter flies away. Obviously you have no idea which way to go. Every direction looks the same. You suddenly realise that you could thrash about in the undergrowth for days without really getting anywhere. You begin to panic. Why is the task of getting to the town virtually impossible? It's because you don't know where you are, and you don't know where you are going.

Now imagine that the helicopter returns to collect you. As it ascends and takes you high above the vegetation, you acquire an aerial view of the whole island. As you gaze down through the window of the helicopter, you can see where you were standing just a few minutes earlier. You can see the sea surrounding the island on all sides. And, most importantly, you can see the town. From your new lofty position you can easily ascertain the direction in which you would have needed to walk to get to your destination.

It's exactly like this with business. While you are frantically busy doing all the everyday tasks deep within the business, you have no time to step back and see what is really happening. Worse, while you are thrashing around in the undergrowth your decisions will be based in undergrowth thinking. Undergrowth thinking is not effective thinking.

To remedy this problem you need to take some time to consider the Big Picture. To access the Big Picture, regularly ask yourself the following questions:

What does my business look like right now?

What do I want my business to look like in one/two/three years?

Is the strategy that I am currently adopting the best way for me to achieve the goal?

Take some time to consider whether your daily actions and activities are the best way to effectively and efficiently get to your desired business outcome. Because without this information you may not only be going down the wrong path, but also you may not realise it's the wrong path until it's too late.

… and the Little Picture

While a frequent mind's eye view of the Big Picture is essential, it is also necessary to be aware of the Little Picture. The Little Picture consists of the small stuff – the things that can so easily go unnoticed when you are frantically doing hard work.

The Little Picture is what's in your immediate vicinity. It's the detail. It's the vital clues that give you invaluable insights into what's working and what isn't.

In the Caribbean island example, while you are frantically hacking your way through virtually impregnable undergrowth with your machete, you may miss something that could be helpful. There might be some barely perceptible footprints that could lead you in a new and useful direction. Or, if you stopped for a few minutes and simply listened, perhaps you might hear the sound of a trickling stream that is just outside of your immediate vision and which you could follow to civilisation.

It's like this in business – while you are busy doing hard work, you will inevitably miss opportunities which, while they are actually all around you, may be just outside of your current range of perception.

For example, one of your customers might provide some feedback which you are too busy to read. In her communication could be a suggestion for an improvement that could be made to one of your products. This improvement could be the key to dramatically increased turnover and profitability.

Or you may miss the chance to take a coffee break with a friend. If you had accepted the invitation, your friend might have told you that he knows someone who has just been let go from their job and would make an excellent assistant in your business.

All the time that you are frantically working in your business, you are like a juggernaut. You have no peripheral vision. There is no time to pick up on the small stuff which could indicate whether you are on the right path, whether you are working effectively, and whether there might be opportunities that you would otherwise miss.

It's a well-reported lore of business that your most successful product will not be your first product. And yet, if you are too busy to pick up the signals that are all around, you will be less likely to spot the opportunity for a second, or third, product.

The Little Picture is vital for business success. But the hard working entrepreneur can easily miss it.

Hard work causes isolation

Hard work is a lonesome activity.

But the hard working entrepreneur doesn't feel lonely, since there is no time to notice the circumstances that would give rise to that feeling. However, she will inevitably spend less time with friends and relatives than before she started down the entrepreneurial path.

The social isolation that comes with hard work is the result of two main factors. The first is that the hard work itself obviously takes time to do. The hours that you are spending doing all the hard work – which may include evenings and weekends – could otherwise be spent having fun with friends. This is self-imposed exile.

The second is that friends and relatives begin to reduce the frequency with which they invite you to their homes, or to social events. To their minds, they are being kind. After all, everyone knows that creating a business is hard work, and caring friends would hardly wish to drag the struggling entrepreneur away from his passion. This is externally imposed exile.

On the rare occasion when you miraculously find some time to spend with other people, your head is likely to be elsewhere – worrying about a business issue or trying to develop a strategy. This 'lack of presence' is hardly conducive to satisfying or fulfilling social encounters. You may just as well not be there.

Slowly and surely you can become more and more isolated, spending less and less time with the important people in your life. Isolation can be comfortably endured only for a relatively short period of time. After prolonged bouts of hard work, life becomes significantly out of balance.

Dedication to hard work, and the social isolation that comes with it, will start to erode your social skills, and your mental acuity will begin to wane. Unfortunately, both of these traits are needed in abundance by the freedom entrepreneur. Hard work therefore results in diminution of the very skills that are so vitally needed for business success.

Worse, the exile that is inevitably inherent in hard work can lead to poor health, the impatience of friends, and to the loss of a spouse or partner. None of that is necessary.

If you are treating hard work as if it's the god of success, it's time for a new deity in your life. It's time to work on your entre-preneurial skills so that you can cease the isolation and begin the process of bringing your life back into balance. For it is only in balance that you can become the freedom entrepreneur.

Hard work disrupts intuition

Intuition is not commonly associated with entrepreneurialism. This may be because we tend to think of business creators as being rational – business decisions are made by weighing specific factors and choosing the most reasonable course of action. Intuition, on the other hand, is based in the less concrete concept of knowing something without there being an obvious and rational reason for the knowledge. Intuition is therefore *irrational*.

There is no doubt that entrepreneurs need to be rational – a rational world requires rational thinking and rational action. But business creators can also benefit from the gifts that intuition brings to the table.

What is intuition?

Intuition is the experience of 'just knowing' that something is right. It's the soft and friendly voice in your head that steers you towards a hitherto untried path or warns you against a particular course of action.

If you've ever had a sense of foreboding, or felt that a way of proceeding was unwise without there being any logic behind it, that is intuition at play.

As well as warning you about possible dangers or inadvisable actions, intuition can lead you in new and exciting directions. It can open up opportunities that you might otherwise not have recognised. It can give you subtle hints at avenues of action that will be abundantly fruitful. Intuition is the unacknowledged hero that sits behind many of mankind's greatest achievements.

Intuition is therefore a most valuable asset for entrepreneurs.

"Intuition will tell the thinking mind where to look next."
– Jonas Salk (polio vaccine discoverer)

And yet, although we have all experienced moments of intuition, we often don't trust them enough to act on their wisdom. Only later, after an unfavourable outcome, do we look back and say "something told me at the time that it wasn't the best thing to do".

Hard work is not our best friend when it comes to utilising the wisdom of intuition. Because it results in a lack of available time to consider the possible merit of intuitive messages. Even if we have a nagging feeling that something is wrong, hard work causes us to ride roughshod over the doubt in the interest of expediency and inertia.

Worse, hard work can remove the possibility of intuitive thoughts arising altogether.

How do we get more intuition?

If we acknowledge that moments of intuition can be very helpful, the most obvious question is how we can obtain more of them.

The problem is that intuition is slippery and obscure. It comes to us when we don't expect it. We can't create it intentionally or summon it into existence. We can't make demands for intuition to tell us how to make a decision or how to resolve a business issue. And, most importantly, we are very unlikely to experience intuition while we are engulfed in hard work.

But although we cannot command intuition to magically arise, we can choose to move into a state of being in which we are ready to receive intuitive messages. We do this by flowing easily with life, rather than rushing. We do it by being open and receptive to what's going on around us, rather than being anxious and agitated. We do it by taking time to be a human just being, rather than a human constantly doing.

Although any form of relaxation will help, meditation and yoga are well known for producing states that give rise to intuition. Exercise can also soften the mind so that it drops into a more intuitive state.

Intuition becomes available when you are physically and mentally well, rather than stressed, happy rather than downhearted, peaceful rather than agitated.

Hard work is therefore anathema to intuition.

Hard work masks your real reasons for becoming an entrepreneur

Here's something that I am certain about: when you were contemplating becoming an entrepreneur, hard work was not one of your main goals.

Hard work is never an aspiration, at least not for its own sake. In fact, if we think about it, working less is probably one of our primary goals. But we make the mistake of assuming that constant hard work is the only route to business success. In doing so, we lose sight of the game plan: the actual reasons why we strived to be entrepreneurial, back at the beginning.

And so, we lose our way.

At the time you contemplated giving up your regular job, perhaps one of your goals was freedom. You wanted to be self-determined. You wanted to be flexible in the way that you make money. You wanted to work where and when you chose to work. Instead of marching to the tune of someone else's clock, you wanted to be in charge of your own day.

But, in the busy-ness, you've lost sight of those goals. You've become a slave to the process.

While you love the fact that you have created a business that serves the needs of its customers as well as making money, you are now working more hours than you ever worked as an employee. In fact, your life as an entrepreneur has become all about work, and therefore significantly out of balance. You've constructed a prison and put yourself firmly behind its bars.

The reality is that you can't achieve your goals by doing ever greater quantities of work. It's time to understand that hard work is a euphemism for poor entrepreneurial skills.

Take a moment to think about your life and your aspirations at the beginning of your entrepreneurial journey. Why did you jump off the conveyor belt? Why did you take the risk?

Was it to increase your wealth? To achieve greater personal autonomy? To have a better lifestyle? To revolutionise an industry? Or simply to show that you could do it?

Now keep your goals in mind.

As you continue on your entrepreneurial path in the present day, keep your mind's eye on the prize, whatever that is for you. And remember that hard work is most definitely not synonymous with success.

Hard work leads to poor decisions

Hard work is stressful. Stress leads to poor decision-making.

The biological effect of hard work on the human body is that it produces stress hormones. Stress hormones force the body into 'survival mode'.

In survival mode, adrenaline is pumped into the heart – enabling heightened awareness and quicker reactivity to possible danger. Blood is rushed to the extremities – enabling either running or fighting. The digestive system closes down – enabling large quantities of energy to be diverted elsewhere. The brain is washed with stress chemicals – enabling very rapid decision-making.

Rapid decision-making may sound ideal, but because the rational brain is closed down in stressful situations, those decisions are based solely on survival modalities. Survival decisions are immediate-term decisions. They are about what is required right now in order to escape imminent harm. These types of decisions are rarely appropriate for longer term business growth.

Therefore, although survival mode can be vital at times of physical danger (facilitating an escape from a charging bear, for example), prolonged exposure to stress hormones causes bad business decisions and unhelpful actions.

When you are in survival mode, you see everything as polar opposites. It's either a good thing, or a bad thing. It's either safe, or it's a threat. It's either your saviour, or your destroyer. It's either black, or it's white.

Let's imagine that, due to a bout of particularly hard work, the stress hormones are raging through your body. Despite being exhausted, the hormones of stress keep you vitally alert. Your ancient lizard brain is hyperactive in its primitive state of survival. Your reasoning and intellectual brain (the neocortex) has closed down, since it's not needed in this mode. Your body is wired and primed for potentially intense and immediate physical action.

You receive an email from a supplier saying that she can no longer make a promised delivery to you this week. How do you react? Most likely your current biological state will force you to interpret the content of the email as a threat. Your lizard brain, which can only choose between fight or flight, decides on the former. You immediately respond with an aggressive email which contains inflammatory and derisive wording.

As it happens, your supplier is also stressed. Her lizard brain interprets your email as a threat to her physical safety, and she tells you that she no longer wishes to do business with you.

The email exchange leaves you in a much worse position than you were previously. Not only do you have the problem of the delayed delivery, but you must now find a new supplier. The stress that was caused by your hard work has resulted in a need for even more work. And so it goes.

Contrary to popular belief, stress does not allow you to get more stuff done. Instead, it creates an environment for your body where your intellectual skills are drastically impaired.

The opposite of stress

Instead of seeing things in black and white, which is the stress condition, we need to view challenges that arise with flexibly and creativity.

Flexibility and creativity are available only in a state of calmness and balance. In this state, the hormones of stress have subsided. The lizard brain goes into hibernation, and your neocortex comes back online. You are able to view circumstances in multiple shades of grey. And, most importantly, you can voluntarily choose to increase the amount of time that passes between the thing that happens and your response to it.

Applying both time and reasoning to any problem will dramatically increase your chances of coming up with a satisfactory result.

Now, in this calm state, imagine that you receive the same email from the supplier. You decide to take some time to consider its content. You realise that she has not specified the reason for the delay. You decide to send her an email which expresses sympathy for her position and enquires how you can help. She tells you that her delivery driver is off sick, whereupon you agree to send someone to her premises to pick up the items.

The freedom entrepreneur values the gap in time between the moment that something happens and the response to it. Because more time between stimulus and response leads to better quality decisions. The bigger the gap, the better the decisions.

The less stressed you are, the larger the gap you can create.

Hard work generates burnout

Every year, thousands of businesses fail. Not because they were poor businesses, but because the founders gave up too early.

They gave up too early because they could not sustain the frantic pace. The quantity of work they were doing simply became too much to bear. For them, the alternative – to return to their pre-entrepreneurial life – became more attractive than living the nightmare they had created.

Giving up their entrepreneurial goals was the price that they had become *glad to pay* for not having to do one more day of hard work.

Winston Churchill famously said, "Never, never, never, never, never give up." It's great advice. But it's not always possible to take this advice. Sometimes things get so tough that you cannot go on. At these times there is no shame in acknowledging our humanity, in making the decision to lay down our tools, and in simply stopping.

For some, it will be a rest and a regrouping, followed by an onward journey. For others it will be the end of the business.

Permanently stepping away from your business aspirations obviously prevents the possibility of a successful enterprise coming into being. It removes from the world the chance for new products or services that would have made a difference. And the jobs and opportunities that would have been created will no longer come into existence.

If going into burnout might lead to the end of your business, then surely it must be better to avoid the hard work which causes it. In order to be able to do this, you need to recognise the signs of approaching burnout. And you must understand that these signs are an urgent warning of impending catastrophe.

Take a look at your current workload. Can you see the signs of approaching burnout? Are you aware that you are spending too much time working? Do you think that hard work is a normal part of business development? Do you feel anxiety and impatience more and more frequently? Do you notice a steadily decreasing amount of time that you are spending in non-work activities? Do you feel your life becoming more and more out of balance? Do you see any of this as a problem?

Whether you can see the final day coming or not, hard work will eventually result in inability to continue onward. Because hard work simply cannot be sustained. Burnout, the eventual result of hard work, is sudden and it's very painful.

But hard work is not necessary. And it is never required. It is entirely possible, and appropriate, to choose the alternative. Instead of working yourself into the ground, you can take time to develop the entrepreneurial skills that are necessary to ensure that you will never experience burnout. You can create a successful business without ever doing any hard work.

Hard work is bad for your health

Health is important. It's probably the most important asset that you have.

Without good health, you lose the ability to fully engage in all the wonders that life makes possible. Without good health, you are not in an optimum condition to look after the people that you care about. Without good health, you become unable to effectively carry out the tasks that will lead to the attainment of your goals.

The problem with hard work is that it diminishes your prospects for good health.

The previous chapter looked at stress in the context of poor decision-making. As far as general health is concerned, we need to remember that stress is a killer. This is because stress causes the human body to become susceptible to breakdown.

We instinctively know that stress is bad for us. But we often choose to ignore it. Especially when we are doing hard work. We might delude ourselves into believing that we are "really not too stressed", or that the stress we are experiencing will be a short-term phenomenon.

But while our bodies are able to deal with (and perhaps even thrive on) short periods of stress, prolonged stress will lead to illness. And that illness may prevent us from carrying out any work at all, let alone hard work.

Quite apart from stress, poor health may also result from a lack of self-care. Hard work reduces the amount of time that is available to you to take measures that are needed for wellness. Wellness requires adequate daily exercise. It requires eating good quality whole and fresh foods. It requires drinking adequate quantities of water. And it requires effective relaxation and sleep time.

Subordinating these wellness essentials to the god of hard work is always misguided.

If we can agree that hard work is a problem because it will very likely lead to poor health, can we also agree that you must choose to take steps to remove or reduce that problem?

Your wellness is essential for your future prosperity. It is difficult to step into the shoes of the freedom entrepreneur without it.

Hard work is addictive

There is no doubt that hard work brings benefits. The problem is that the acquisition of the benefits can become addictive. When that happens, the need for hard work becomes self-reinforcing.

Another type of addiction that arises from hard work is escapism. This happens when hard work allows us to remove ourselves from something that we don't like.

Let's look at some examples of these two types of addiction.

Addiction to benefits

Acquiring new customers is a clear benefit. What could be more gratifying, and more compelling, than new purchasers of our wares? Another benefit is a steadily increasing bank balance. What could be a more delightful pay-off for our hard work than a growing level of income?

Each of these events makes us *feel* better. Our bodies produce symptoms of pleasure. The 'hit' that we get from each new customer, or each bank balance increment, can therefore result in a chemical addiction to work. Especially if we believe that working harder will result in more hits (or if we believe that working less will result in fewer hits).

There are two things to understand about this type of addiction to hard work. The first is that it's not real. It's a mistake to believe that the benefits of running a business can only be achieved by hard work. The truth is that all of the benefits can be achieved in other ways.

The second is that we become gradually more and more accustomed to the pleasurable sensations that we associate with the benefits of hard work. As we become more and more accustomed, their effect diminishes. The pleasure that you experience reduces over time. In other words, each high takes more and more hard work to achieve. Pretty soon you need three new customers just to get the same feeling that one new customer previously provided.

And so our *need* for hard work increases over time. An ever-increasing need for hard work is unsustainable.

Addiction to escapism

Addiction also arises when hard work allows us to hide from something. Because when we engage in all-consuming hard work, we cannot do anything else. If hard work is substantially preferable to the other thing, then it will become addictive.

For example, we may be facing an issue with a spouse or partner that we know needs addressing but which we don't want to tackle. Or a problem with our house or car that really needs our attention, but which we would rather not look into. Or a personal health issue that we hope will go away.

We can, apparently quite legitimately, say to others and ourselves, "I'm too busy with work to spend time on that issue." The problem is that those issues may be important for us to deal with. Failing to handle them may result in a breakdown in an area of our lives which is vital for our continued wellbeing.

Any type of hard work is unsustainable in the longer term. Hard work fuelled by escapism is doubly dangerous since it prevents the taking of necessary action in other areas of our lives.

If hard work has become an addiction, what can be done?

First, you need to acknowledge that your addiction to hard work, if it remains unchecked, will eventually end in some kind of disaster.

Next, acknowledge that you have been mistaken all along. Hard work is not necessary in order to acquire customers or to make more money. And hiding from important issues will never make them go away – it simply delays the inevitable day of reckoning, and often makes the original issue worse.

Then, take some time to think about what is really going on – what are you gaining, or hiding from, by dint of the hard work?

Finally, you must choose a different path. One such path is the one proposed in this book.

Take a look at the following questions:

> *What problems do I have in my life that I am avoiding by working hard?*
>
> *If I am using hard work as escapism, what am I trying to escape from?*
>
> *Am I using hard work as a sedative to numb the pain that I would otherwise feel, and if so what would that pain be caused by?*
>
> *What scares me about sitting quietly, calmly and un-distractedly in an armchair?*
>
> *Do I need to take some action in other areas of my life so that hard work is not such an addiction for me?*
>
> *Could I still achieve the 'highs' that hard work seems to bring by having someone else do the work?*

Remember that the life of the freedom entrepreneur is a life that is in balance. A life in balance contains no compulsive, or addictive, behaviour.

Therefore, it may be time to acknowledge that it is more important for your future success to stop the hard work, and instead deal with the issues that cause hard work to be so attractive.

Consider whether hard work is actually a perceived antidote to your greatest fear. If it is, it may be time to contemplate the fear, to sit with it for a while. As Yoda said, "*Named must your fear be, before banish it you can*." While we all have fears, indulging in hard work to avoid them does you no favours, and will eventually result in burnout.

Hard work diminishes creativity

Your business consists of ideas. Mostly, these are ideas that you yourself have had.

As a successful entrepreneur, one of your greatest accolades is your proven ability to put your ideas into practice. Your ideas, plus your desire and willingness to take action on your ideas, is the reason that you have achieved business success so far. It is the key distinguishing feature that makes you different from most other people.

But let's take a step back for a moment. In order to be able to take action on an idea, you needed to have the idea in the first place.

In fact, if you think about it, the original foundation for your success is all about the ideas that you have had. Ideas about the type of business that you would run. Ideas for attracting customers. Ideas about promoting your products and services. Ideas for how your business would function on a daily basis. Ideas about manufacturing or production processes. Ideas for the locations in which your business would operate.

Your business consists of the realisation of your ideas. If you had no ideas, you would have no business.

But the need for ideas doesn't stop at the start-up phase. Although the ideas that you had for your business in the early days were essential to the creation of your business, it is fundamentally important to your future success that you continue to be creative. In other words, ideas today are just as important to your success as they were at the start of your business journey. In order to remain successful, you must nurture your invaluable ability to generate ideas.

The problem is that the more successful your business becomes (and the harder you work as a result), the fewer ideas you have. Why does this happen? It's because the environment that is generated by hard work is anathema to creativity.

Monkey mind prevents ideas

Instead of promoting the flow of ideas, hard work creates 'monkey mind'.

Monkey mind is a phrase that Buddhists use to describe a state of mental agitation. It occurs when there is an uncontrollable stream of thoughts in rapid succession.

In monkey mind, your thinking is so fast and erratic that it becomes jumbled and obscure. If you wanted to put yourself into the state of experiencing monkey mind, one way to do it would be to overload yourself with urgent tasks that have unrealistic deadlines. Doing hard work will therefore cause monkey mind, leading to less creativity and less entrepreneurial effectiveness.

A reduction in creativity is a problem since creativity is vital in order to produce effective methods of working, to come up with new ideas for products and services, and to find innovative solutions to tricky problems.

Monkey mind removes your ability to handle situations effectively, because it causes you to behave like a rabbit caught in headlights.

How do we avoid, or at least lessen the occurrences of, monkey mind?

We do it by taking time away from work, and from worry about work. We do it by allowing ourselves the luxury of relaxation. It's not possible to be relaxed at the same time as experiencing monkey mind.

Ideas best come when you are relaxed

Take a look at your own past great ideas. When do you tend to have them? Is it while you are working hard? Or is it while you are relaxing in the sunshine on a beach, taking a walk with your dog, jogging in the park, hiking in a thick forest, or feeling warm water drenching your body in the shower?

Sometimes as entrepreneurs we forget how to relax. Personally, I am very fond of doing exactly nothing – not for its own sake, but for the sake of business development. The idea that doing nothing can assist you in your entrepreneurial endeavours can seem surprising. But my experience is that it does just that. Franz Kafka, the Austro-Hungarian philosopher, says it best: "*You do not need to leave your room. Remain sitting at your table and listen. Do not even listen, simply wait, be quiet and still, and solitary… The world will freely offer itself to you to be unmasked. It has no choice; it will roll in ecstasy at your feet.*"

What Kafka is describing, I believe, is the notion that ideas and solutions to problems can spontaneously occur to you as a result of the space that is opened up by injecting periods of complete relaxation into your day.

Hard work, on the other hand, will remove these potential benefits from your experience.

Hard work is self-perpetuating

The combination of each of the factors described in Part One creates an environment in which the business creator is at the mercy of events.

Rather than being centred and grounded, he is frantic and hyperactive. Rather than being the master of his own destiny, the hard working entrepreneur is constantly being blown off course and distracted. Rather than having clarity of thought and freedom of movement, he is constrained and restricted.

In this way, hard work creates the very circumstances from which it is almost impossible to escape.

There is another way.

Part Two

Thinking as the Freedom Entrepreneur

"Whether you think you can,
or you think you can't,
you are right."
– HENRY FORD

Stop thinking like an employee

Most entrepreneurs suffer from an unseen and unacknowledged problem. It's that they don't think like entrepreneurs. Instead they think like employees. This is not surprising, because it's what they were trained to do.

The entrepreneur's past

People who go into business usually have no background or experience in running a business. In most cases, people who start a business have just stopped working for someone else. They were hairdressers or lawyers, graphic designers or accountants, plumbers or investment bankers, doctors or belly dancers, nutritionists or recruiters, yoga teachers or dive instructors. And they had a dream of doing it for themselves, rather than for someone else.

There is nothing wrong with that aspiration. The problem is that there is a huge difference between being a chef and running a restaurant. The skills needed, and most importantly the *way of thinking* that is required for success, are radically different.

As an employee, we come to understand that success is a product of hard work. For the entrepreneur, on the other hand, the amount of success that you achieve is proportionate to how dedicated you are to the acquisition of entrepreneurial skills. The outcome of such dedication is not hard work – it's the opposite.

The way forward

The purpose of Part One was to demonstrate that hard work is entirely counter-productive for entrepreneurs. Rather than hastening our goal of business success, hard work wrenches us further away from our aspirations.

*"80% of success in life is psychological,
20% is mechanics."*
– Tony Robbins

Part Two begins to lay the foundations for an alternative to hard work. It starts with making a change in the way that you think about yourself and your business.

Before getting to that, let's take a look at *why* you have been doing hard work. You need to know this so that you can successfully and sustainably leave hard work firmly in your past.

The reason that you have been doing hard work is most likely because you believed that you had to. And, despite having read Part One, you probably still believe that. So we need to go to work on your beliefs. Because beliefs lead to behaviour.

The tricky thing about our behaviour is that it's not driven by what we *know*; it is driven by what we *believe*. Belief is deeper than knowledge. What you know is simply facts, whereas what you believe is the basis of your own personal reality. Simply changing your knowledge will not necessarily result in a change in your behaviour.

For example, you may learn that eating sugar is bad for your health. But that knowledge may not necessarily result in you eating less chocolate.

Similarly, being told that you must work less in order to achieve more business success will not be sufficient on its own to change your way of working.

To sustainably change behaviour, you need to go further than simply learning new stuff. You need to take a look at what you think. Because if you think something often enough, it will become a belief. In this way, what you most regularly contemplate becomes your reality. And your own version of reality leads to the actions that you take.

"All is as thinking makes it so."
– Marcus Aurelius

Hard work

Let's take a look at hard work as an example. It is generally considered by most people, as concrete *fact*, that the only way to achieve business success is by engaging in hard work. If you are going to believe the opposite – that hard work is your nemesis – then you need to ditch a belief that you have probably held for your entire life.

Part Two of this book challenges the conventional wisdom that hard work is essential for business success. It also attempts to debunk a few other mainstream beliefs. And it invites you to take a look at some possible alternatives to those beliefs. It may be a bumpy ride because you will come up against the entrepreneur's greatest foe: resistance to change. Remember that the objective, as for everything in the book, is to enable you to step into the shoes of the freedom entrepreneur. Changing your beliefs cannot be done *merely* by learning new stuff.

Your business

Let's take a look at your business. It may be obvious that the way that you are currently thinking about your business has a direct influence on it. After all, your business consists of the actions and decisions you take, and those actions and decisions are derived from your beliefs, which in turn are derived from your frequent thoughts. So the influences that you bring to bear on your business in the present effectively create your future business. In other words, your thinking, in each moment, has a significant influence on all your future moments. You literally create your future from your thinking.

Therefore it is vitally important to have an awareness of what you are thinking in the current moment. Once you become aware of your thinking, you can then see if it is aligned with your business aspirations.

If what you are thinking is not congruent with massive business growth coupled with a dramatic reduction in your own

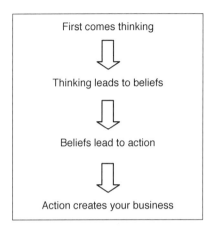

First comes thinking

⬇

Thinking leads to beliefs

⬇

Beliefs lead to action

⬇

Action creates your business

workload, then it is likely that you are unwittingly working against your own success. In which case, you will need to adjust your thinking so that it becomes aligned with what you are aiming to achieve.

As an example, take a look at the beliefs of Entrepreneur A and Entrepreneur B in the box 'Possible Types of Thinking'. Which of the two entrepreneurs, A or B, do you think is more likely to succeed in creating a flourishing and sustainable business?

Possible Types of Thinking	
Entrepreneur A	*Entrepreneur B*
Success is always elusive – just when you think you have a handle on it, it slips out of your grasp.	Success is most certainly achievable for those who are willing to learn what it takes to be successful.
Money is scarce and difficult to acquire.	Money is constantly circulating – it is abundant and easily attainable.
Taking on staff is a waste of time. People never do a good job and they are more trouble than they are worth.	Most people want to do a good job. They simply need the tools and appropriate guidance with which to do it.
I must consistently be a tough and aggressive operator in order to succeed.	I need to pay close attention to people and circumstances in order to be successful.

I'm fairly certain that you chose Entrepreneur B as being more likely to succeed. The reason that you chose Entrepreneur B is because you instinctively know that the way that a person thinks has a direct influence on their future reality.

But, I hear you protest, surely I can't change the way that I think! Surely thinking is a fixed part of a person's personality which can't be controlled!

The good news is that is incorrect. Thinking is not immutable.

If you think about it, you will see that your thinking changes over time, as you personally evolve. You may no longer think the same way that you did ten years ago. The even better news is that you can choose to take steps, right now, to change the way that you think. All it takes is a willingness to be open to possible new thoughts. Try this:

> *Close your eyes and, for the next thirty seconds, think about the best vacation you ever had.*

How did you get on? My bet is that you were successful, at least for part of the thirty seconds. If I hadn't asked you to think about the best vacation you ever had, you would have thought about something else during that period of time. Instead you changed your own thinking. You can do this any time. You just need to remember to do it. And, as with all skills, practise is essential. The more you throw a spanner into your standard mental programming, the more that the type of thinking that you want to produce will become normal for you.

> *"You have to work hard to get your thinking clean to make it simple."*
> – STEVE JOBS

The remaining chapters in Part Two are about changing your thinking so that your actions will become aligned with those of the freedom entrepreneur. Keep an open mind while you are reading, and practise adapting your thinking so that you begin to develop the following beliefs:

- Great results can be achieved by working effectively

- Being successful is about developing entrepreneurial skills

- I can serve more customers, and therefore make more money, by delegating effectively to others

- The amount of time that I work has no direct bearing on the success or failure of my business

Think of yourself separately from your business

Business creators often confuse themselves with their business.

If you are a hard working entrepreneur, you are very likely to think of your business as either yourself or as part of yourself. The freedom entrepreneur, on the other hand, always sees her business as being *separate* from herself.

Thinking that your business is part of you can be a very costly error. Because it creates a massive psychological barrier to your business's growth potential. This chapter explains why the confusion is a problem, and what to do about it.

Problems with the confusion

There are several reasons that it's necessary for you to mentally separate yourself from your business.

The first is that you need to remove emotion from business decisions. Because allowing your feelings to colour your reactions leads to poorly thought out choices.

For example, suppose a supplier sends you shoddy merchandise. You are unable to use the product in the business, but when you contact the supplier for a refund, he refuses to speak with you. How will you react?

As for all business decisions, it is necessary for you to evaluate the situation with a cool head. You must figure out what is *best for the business*. However, if you see the business as yourself, you might take the situation *personally*. This could cause you to devote too much energy on obtaining the refund. Dwelling on the 'unfairness' of the situation may keep you awake at night. How dare the supplier treat you this way! Doesn't he understand that it's wrong to supply duff products? Doesn't he know who he is dealing with?

If matters get very fraught, you might take a decision to sue the supplier. There is nothing wrong with starting a legal action in appropriate circumstances. But you need to remove the emotion from the decision-making process.

The way to remove the emotional element is to see the business as being entirely separate from you. The supplier has done nothing to *you*. Instead, he has supplied shoddy merchandise to *the business*. When you examine the situation with coolness and detachment you may see that the value of the refund is relatively small. You may realise that the time and energy that it would take to obtain the refund could be better (and more profitably) spent on growing your business. Removing the emotion from business decisions is a vital skill of the freedom entrepreneur.

Second, confusing yourself with your business will make it difficult for you to develop a skill which is vital for business growth: this is the skill of delegation (we look at delegation in Part Six). Without the ability to delegate, you will be personally forced to do more and more work, until you can work no more. That leads to burnout. You don't need to go there.

Third, thinking of yourself and your business as essentially the same thing will tie together your personal wellbeing and the success, or failure, of your business. Each happening within the business that is good news (for example, obtaining a new customer that you have always wanted), will result in you feeling better about yourself. Each negative occurrence (for example, having to pay a supplier more money than you anticipated) will feel like a mini stab in the heart. This is a rollercoaster of emotion that you cannot afford to ride. The freedom entrepreneur knows that she must keep her composure during the business creation journey.

The fourth, and by far the most important, reason that you must see the business as being a wholly separate entity from yourself, is that you must be able to imagine the business working when you are not. If you conflate yourself and your business, then the business only works when you do – this is not appropriate for your non-hard working future self. The business must be able to function when you are on vacation, or playing sports, or walking the dog, or just doing nothing.

In order to move away from identifying with your business, you need to draw a line in the sand. You are you, a living breathing human being. Your business is something that you have created. In other words, to become the freedom entrepreneur, you must understand, and actually *believe*, that: you are not your business.

Towards an amicable separation

So, from today, you must start to look at your business as being separate from yourself. After all, you and your business have different needs, engage in different activities, and have different goals.

How do you alter your thinking so that you see your business as separate from yourself? How do you give yourself the flexibility to choose actions for your business that are primarily compatible with the needs of your business? And to take actions for yourself that are primarily compatible with your own needs?

If you think about it, it's obvious that you and your business are different entities. You are a human being, and your business is ... well, your business.

If you happen to run your business using a limited company, the distinction is more obvious. Lawyers refer to a company as being a 'separate legal entity'. The company has a life of its own – it was born when it became incorporated, and it will live until it is wound up. The life of your company does not coincide with your own lifespan. When your business becomes successful, you may choose to sell it – it's not *you* that you are selling.

But not all businesses are run via a limited company. You may run your business as a sole trader (or as a self-employed person) or in partnership with other people. In each of these cases it's just as important that you understand, and believe, that the business is separate from you.

Minding your language

The way you think (about everything) is displayed for all to hear in the words that you use. This is because your thinking leads to your choice of language.

Most people understand, even if only subconsciously, that the words people use disclose their mental state and their view of reality.

The freedom entrepreneur understands a deeper truth. Which is that it's also true the other way around. In other words, your language creates your thinking. This means that your words produce your personal reality.

For example, if you constantly use gloomy words when you are speaking with people, you will start to feel down and low on energy. Conversely, a proliferation of cheerful words will lead to an upbeat disposition.

Since you are in total control of the way that you speak, you have access to a powerful tool to build your future as you wish it to be.

Knowing this means that you can choose words and phrases that make it clear, to yourself as well as to others, that you see your business as being separate from yourself.

For example, instead of saying "I'm experiencing some great business growth at the moment", say "my business is growing well at the moment".

Instead of saying "I'm working too much", say "my business is taking up too much of my time".

Use phraseology that draws a clear distinction between you and your business in order to give yourself the entrepreneurial advantage.

Separating the money

New entrepreneurs, especially hard working ones, forget to draw a distinction between their own money and their business's money. It's important to understand that these are two separate sets of finances.

Take a look at your own financial situation. How do you handle business money? When customers make a payment, where does the money go? If it goes into your own bank account, this will not help you to view your business as being separate from yourself.

Take steps to open a bank account for your business money. And ensure that the money within the business account always stays separate from your own finances.

Of course a steadily accumulating pool of money can be attractive when you are personally in need of funds. No problem. You can take a loan from the business, or pay yourself a bonus or dividend. If you take a loan, remember that the loan is outstanding, and ensure that the business is repaid when you are in a position to pay it back.

Using different space

An excellent method to cement the distinction between yourself and your business in your thinking is to separate your life space from your business space. Don't do life stuff in the business space. And don't do business stuff in the life space.

If you work from home, use a separately designated room for your business. If you don't have a whole room available, use a different part of the room for your work.

If you have a separate office or other premises where you do business work, don't work at home. This can be challenging – especially when you are at home and you suddenly remember that you need to send an email – but keeping the distinction is a great way for you to think like the freedom entrepreneur. And it will lead to better work/life balance.

Thinking about what's best for the business (and what's best for you)

Actions that are best for you will sometimes be different from actions that are best for your business. And vice versa.

Whenever you are about to make a business decision, take a moment to ensure that you prioritise what is best for the business, as opposed to what is best for you.

Conversely, when you are making a personal decision, make sure that you consider what is best for you over and above the needs of your business.

This type of separate thinking is not easy at first, and can seem rather odd. Especially because it will mean that you will sometimes be required to make business decisions that are not so good for you personally. And you will need to take actions in your personal life that may be detrimental to your business. That is as it must be – it is the discipline of the freedom entrepreneur.

For example, you may feel unwell. Making the decision to take some time off work for recuperation may be the best thing for you. The time off in the short term will allow you to get well more quickly than if you didn't rest. It's not so good for the business because taking time off means that you are unavailable to handle business issues.

Or your business may develop a product or expertise that requires it to be located elsewhere. Although it's not so great for you personally, you decide to move your home so that your business can take advantage of the opportunities.

Use a different name

If possible, choose a name for your business that does not contain your own name.

Although there may be some good reasons for choosing to name your business after yourself, it will not help you to see the business as being separate from you.

If your business name does contain all or part of your own name, it's not the end of the world. But it will mean that you'll have to pay greater attention to your thinking. You will need to keep reminding yourself that you are not your business.

If an opportunity arises to change the name of your business, choose a name that is not currently associated with you.

Money – Part 1
(making money is not wrong)

As human beings, money is one of our biggest challenges.

As a topic of conversation, the subject of money takes up more time than any other. As a source of worry and fear, it's the primary cause. As a reason for the breakdown of human relationships, it's the commonest one. As a ground for business failure, it's the most usual. As a source of unhappiness, nothing can compare with the deep despair caused by the subject of money.

As Douglas Adams remarked in *The Hitchhiker's Guide to the Galaxy*, "*This planet has ... a problem, which [is] this: most of the people living on it [are] unhappy for pretty much of the time. Many solutions were suggested for this problem, but most of these were largely concerned with the movement of small green pieces of paper, which [is] odd because on the whole it wasn't the small green pieces of paper that were unhappy.*"

In my view, our unhappiness about money is caused by a mis-understanding about what money actually is. An economist once said: "Money is just a tool." If we actually believed this truth, we would be much better business people.

Money is important

There is no doubt that money is a vitally important topic for business creators. Here are some reasons why:

- We work on building our business for money – we want a great lifestyle for ourselves and for the people that we care about. Money can't buy happiness, but it goes a long way towards it.

- We get judged on how much money we make – people gauge our success as entrepreneurs on the ability of our business to make money. The more money our business makes, the more successful it is. On the other side of that coin, if our business doesn't make money, it's regarded as a failure (even if its products or services are excellent).

- We feel pressure to make money – the pressure comes not only from ourselves, but also from other people whose opinions we value.

So, money is at the very heart of what we do. And, while money must never be the *only* goal in being an entrepreneur, it is an essential part of the big entrepreneurial picture.

The problem comes when the way that we *think* about money holds us back from being freedom entrepreneurs. Because our thinking about money is the biggest determinant as to whether we will be successful at making money.

Incorrect thinking about money

Some entrepreneurs have a deeply held belief that making money is somehow wrong or bad. Many of these entrepreneurs think that they don't think this way. In other words, many people have a sub-conscious and insidious belief that it is inappropriate to want to make money.

Take a look at these statements and see if you agree with any of them:

Having lots of money means that you are greedy

Money is the root of all evil

To be rich, you have to use people and take advantage of them

It's not right for me to be wealthy while others in the world have nothing

Money corrupts people

It's more spiritual to be poor than wealthy

Do any of these beliefs sound familiar? If just one of these statements matches your own way of thinking, then you are setting yourself up for failure. Because having one of these types of beliefs creates an internal conflict.

On the surface, you take actions and decisions that are consistent with building a money-making business. But hidden beneath the obvious, your unspoken belief that making money is wrong or bad is silently sabotaging your every effort.

If this sounds like your own beliefs, continue reading this chapter. If not, you can skip to the next chapter.

Money as a hammer

If you believe that wanting to make money is somehow bad, then you will need to adjust your thinking so that you stop creating conflict between your actions and your thinking.

In order to do this, you need to reassess your understanding of money. You must start to accept that money is nothing more than a tool. Just like, for example, a hammer.

A hammer is not a bad thing in itself. It could be used to build a house. On the other hand, it could be used to kill a person. The tool itself is neutral. It's what's done with it that counts.

It's the same thing with money – it's neither good, nor bad.

Once you have fully developed the belief that money is simply a tool, the idea that making money could be wrong or bad will evaporate.

Michael's views on money

Michael was a successful entrepreneur, who worked too hard.

After experiencing burnout, he set about looking into where he had gone wrong. He realised that the cause of his burnout was partly rooted in internal conflict about money.

After some self-analysis, he discovered the reason for his negative beliefs about money. He had grown up in a relatively poor environment, and he had attended a school for kids who were mostly from poor backgrounds. He remembered that whenever the kids saw a display of wealth in the world, they would be disparaging.

For example, when they saw an expensive car driving by, they would mock the driver, and even shout insults at him or her. People who had achieved success were regarded as crooks. And people who lived in large houses were 'different', and therefore inappropriate to hang out with.

All of this conditioning caused Michael to have a strong sub-conscious pull in the direction of poverty. He believed, at a deep level, that it was neither cool nor socially acceptable to have wealth.

Michael needed to go to work on his own reality around money. He needed to reprogramme his thinking so that he was able to see the benefits of having money. In order to counteract the deep negative beliefs, he needed to engage in this reprogramming on a regular basis.

Each morning for six weeks, Michael made a list of the things that he could do with a large amount of money, if he had it. The point of this exercise was to get himself to believe that making money could be positive and beneficial. Because of all the fabulous and wonderful things that could be done with it.

As he made the lists consistently each day, his negativity around the subject of money began to slowly dissipate. The space that arose where the negativity had previously existed allowed new, more positive, thoughts about money to enter his mind.

As his negative beliefs grew less strong, he started to see how making money could be a good thing. In stark contrast to the anguished period of time prior to burnout, he started to see more clearly the growth possibilities for his business.

Doing this exercise over an extended period gave him a new empowering perspective on the acquisition of money. He realised that if his business made more profit, he could afford to take on employees. And he could afford to pay them well, and to provide them with generous vacation time. He began to visualise paying dividends to the company's shareholders – it was exciting to contemplate being generous.

This exercise had two beneficial effects on Michael's personal thinking. The first was to produce a belief that making money could be a positive experience. The second was that he began to feel excited about the changes that he could implement in his life if he had more money. He found that this opening up of possibilities, combined with the emotion of excitement, was a very powerful and motivating force. He returned to his business newly invigorated and excited.

Feeling guilty about wanting to make money

When thinking about making money, some entrepreneurs feel guilt.

Although this is not uncommon, it is always mistaken. Because it's based on a false premise. The false premise is that some of the things that you want to do with the money are wrong or bad.

If you suffer from feelings of guilt around wanting to make money, then you need to adjust your thinking so that you think thoughts that are more helpful to your aspirations. You need to reinterpret your desires.

The freedom entrepreneur is always conscious of the positive things that can be done with money.

If Michael's situation is familiar to you, or if you feel guilty about wanting money, try this exercise:

Money Exercise 1

Each morning for the next two weeks, make a list of positive things you could do with a large amount of money. Part of the objective of this exercise is to have some fun around the subject of money. Feel free to be outrageous with your choices. Don't censor yourself or restrict your-

self in any way – just make a list of whatever comes to your mind.

For example, you might buy a Ferrari.

Or pay off your parents' mortgage.

Or send a donation to your favourite charity.

Or move into a bigger apartment.

Or buy a boat.

Or pay for your friends to go on a trip.

Or buy a diamond ring.

It doesn't really matter what things you write, as long as they are exciting for you. Never judge yourself on the contents of your list. Whatever is on your list is totally fine. Just keep making the lists each day.

Once you have identified what you think, and feel, about money, doing this exercise every day will automatically adjust your thinking so that your new beliefs will better serve your business aspirations. The object here is not to banish the unhelpful beliefs and feelings completely (that might take years of therapy!), but to reduce their negative impact on you.

Remember, it's not wrong for you to want to acquire money. You are not a bad person for going after wealth. Wanting money is no different from wanting anything else. It's simply a choice. No judgement. No guilt. No problem.

Money – Part 2
(making money is not difficult)

Many people believe that making money is difficult.

Such people might best be dissuaded from becoming entrepreneurs. Unless they are willing to go to work on their self-limiting beliefs.

Remember Henry Ford's quote at the beginning of this Part – essentially, he was saying that the world is exactly as you think it is. It's the same thing with money. Making money is exactly as difficult, for you, as you believe.

The problem is that adjusting our thinking about money can seem more challenging than adjusting our thinking about other things. This is because when we think about money, the concept comes with baggage. This baggage consists of the thoughts and feelings that we have about money.

For example, if we think that we don't have enough money, we *feel* something. That feeling usually incorporates a negative self-image. "I am unworthy of having money." "I am a poor business person." "Money doesn't like me." If we think and feel those things often enough, we will associate them with money itself. So then every time we think about money, we feel the negative emotion associated with it.

When thinking about money produces a negative emotional response, it's inevitable that we will be uncomfortable about money. And thinking that causes an emotional response becomes more ingrained than thinking to which we are less attached.

Some people are so uncomfortable about money that they regard the subject of money as being inappropriate for polite conversation.

If we agree that business is mostly about making money, then we must agree that a person who is uncomfortable around the subject of money will not be well-equipped to take the decisions that are necessary to make money.

Being entirely at ease with thinking about, and discussing, the subject of making money is a prerequisite to being the freedom entrepreneur.

Your beliefs about money become your reality

Whatever you truly believe, deep down, about money will be the reality of your experience of money (remember that beliefs come from recurrent thinking).

If you often think that money is difficult to come by, then it will be that for you. If you think that money is plentiful and easy to acquire, then that will become your reality.

Therefore we want to adapt your thinking so that it makes it easier for you to become the freedom entrepreneur. This involves two steps. The first step is to avoid thoughts that lead to beliefs that money is a rare and elusive commodity, or that it's inappropriate for you to have more of it. Below are examples of some of these types of thinking. As you read them, think about how having any one of these beliefs could sabotage your business aspirations.

Having lots of money means that you are greedy

Money is the root of all evil

Making money is difficult

To be rich, you have to use people and take advantage of them

Toiling for money can cause stress and lead to health problems

It's not right for me to be wealthy while others in the world have nothing

Being successful is all about luck

There is no point in making more money, since I will then have to pay more tax

Money is not really important

Money corrupts people

It's very difficult to be a successful entrepreneur

Most of the good opportunities are already gone

None of these statements are 'true'. They are all opinions that some people have, and other people do not. An entrepreneur who has any one (or more) of these beliefs will be doing battle against themselves every time they go to work on their business.

The second step is to promote thoughts that lead to beliefs that money is plentiful and abundant. Here are some examples:

There are always business opportunities

Governments are printing money every day

There is enough wealth in the world to feed the population a million times over

Everything is in abundance

Take some time to consider your own limiting beliefs about money. What are alternative thoughts that you could practise instead?

The real nature of money

In reality money is simply a tool to help us to trade more easily.

If you make or build something of value, you can sell it and take the proceeds to the supermarket to purchase food – you don't have to take the thing you made to the store and swap it for milk and eggs.

The problem arises when we think that money is more than just a tool.

We might see money as standing for security, power, success, respect, sexual attractiveness, status, glamour or personal esteem.

In other words, we can associate money with something that we find desirable. In doing so, we become attached to the thing that we think money is. This is a problem because the attachment leads to an emotional response. This emotional response can prevent us taking effective business decisions.

For example, if you think that a recent payment of money into your business represents an increase in your personal status, you may be unwilling to spend that money on a product that would make your business more productive. Your emotional attachment to what the money represents to you (status), rather than what the money actually is (a tool), will get in the way of your effectiveness. You want to maintain the bank balance rather than invest the money for better business opportunities.

Money Exercise 2

What associations do you have with money? Make a list of them. Take a look at your list frequently and, for each item on the list, tell yourself that money is not that. It is simply a trading device. This will help you begin to erode your own self-destructive beliefs about money.

Be unreasonable

How many times have you experienced someone telling you to be reasonable? "Jack, why don't you be more reasonable in your aspirations?" Other words that people use to make themselves feel more comfortable are "realistic", "sensible", "practical" and "appropriate".

For you to become the freedom entrepreneur, what we want instead is for you to be the opposite of reasonable. We want you to be unreasonable. Unreasonable in this context means unrealistic, or outlandish.

Try this exercise:

Money Exercise 3

Think about how much money your business can reasonably make, if everything goes well, by this time next year. Now multiply that number by 10. The new figure is unreasonable! Write it down. Think about this figure every day. Treat it as a game rather than as a serious endeavour – by not taking it too seriously, your brain won't try to come up with all the reasons why it's 'impossible' to achieve. Just have fun with thinking about how your life will look when your business is making that amount of money.

By continually contemplating your business making an unreasonable amount of money, you will find that your mind inevitably begins to shift in its thinking. Instead of dismissing the amount as ridiculous, you will notice that you will start to consider (almost sub-consciously) how it could be possible.

Your mind will be in contemplation of the new unreasonable figure and will start to wonder how on Earth the business could have made so much money – it will look at the outrageous future figure and start to work backwards in time. By that I mean that your mind will attempt to work out what would have had to have happened, between now and the future time, so that such a huge amount of business success was actually achieved.

For example, how many staff would you have needed to take on? What size office space would you have needed? How many more customers would you have acquired? What type of marketing would you have needed to have done? How open in your thinking would you have needed to have been?

The result of this exercise is that your brain begins to see the unreasonable as being possible. And that is all that you need. Just enough tweaking in your beliefs to move your thinking away from 'definitely impossible' to 'vaguely possible' is all that is required to pave the way.

Have fun with being unreasonable, and see what happens.

Money – Part 3
(making money needs an end point)

Despite the importance of money, there is a key question which most entrepreneurs never ask themselves. This is unfortunate because not knowing the answer to this question leads to hard work and burnout.

The question is this: *how much is enough?*

This question has a subjective answer. It's about how much is enough *for you*.

No one can answer this question for you. There is no right answer. There is no wrong answer. The answer is whatever you want it to be (and you can change it whenever you like).

But you must calculate it.

Because the problem with never coming up with an answer is this: unless you know how much money is enough, you will never be able to stop going after more.

Only by having an actual figure in mind will you know when your financial goal has been achieved. If you don't know whether you have enough, you consign yourself to more and more work … forever.

We've all heard of workaholic millionaires who continue toiling excessively until the end of their lives. There is no freedom down that road.

Instead, we want you to be able to say, "I've done it! I now have enough. I have succeeded." At that point, you will have the luxury of being able to choose your future path. You can continue to grow your business, if you want to. Or not.

So let's take a look at how much is enough for you.

Calculating enough

In order to get to 'enough', we need to know what it means.

The enough that we are trying to achieve is a regular stream of income which is sufficient to provide you with your ideal lifestyle. The stream of income will come from one of two (or both) sources:

• Profits of your business – this is money that is left over for you after all expenses have been paid

• Investment income – this is income that comes from investments that you purchased using money that came from your business profits or from the sale of your business

> *"All money means to me is a*
> *pride in accomplishment."*
> – RAY KROC (CREATIVE FORCE BEHIND McDONALD'S)

In either case, the income will be either active or passive. Active income is money that you make as a direct result of work that you do. Passive income is money that you receive in the absence of any work undertaken by you.

Passive income is the holy grail of the freedom entrepreneur.

Either of the above two categories of income stream could include passive income. But in the case where the money comes from recurrent profits, true passive income requires that you are no longer working in the business.

Said another way, you need to have one of the following two goals in mind:

1. To sell your business for an amount that will generate sufficient income for your ideal lifestyle

2. To grow your business until the profits that it generates are sufficient for your ideal lifestyle

How much is enough?

The best way to find out how much is enough is to figure out the ingredients of your ideal lifestyle. Then work out how much you would need annually in order to afford that lifestyle.

Use the following exercise to find your number:

Money Exercise 4

Think about your ideal life – how your life will look, and what you will be doing, when your business is successful and you have lots of free time. Down the left hand side of a page/screen, make a list of each item that comprises this lifestyle. Include all the usual expenses of living, such as rent/mortgage payments, energy and communications bills, travel to work, school fees and food costs. Also include your choice of luxury items, such as the number of long haul flights, your preferred type of second home, choice of boat and ideal mooring, quantity of dinners out, contributions to your favourite charity and gifts to friends and family. Make sure that your list is as comprehensive as possible and ensure that you have included all the elements of your perfect life. Have fun with it. Don't hold back. Don't fall into the trap of trying to be 'realistic' or 'reasonable'. Then, against each item, insert the approximate annual cost. Make a calculation of the total, and insert the figure at the bottom of the column of numbers.

Once you have calculated the total annual expenditure figure, you will know how much profit your business (or your investments, if you are going to sell your business) will need to generate annually.

When your business (or investments) has achieved the level of sufficient income production to meet your needs, including all of the luxury items you have listed, you will have made it!

At that stage, there will be no *need* to grow the business further. And so you will have a choice – to relax and enjoy the success that you have achieved, or to continue to grow the business for even higher results. The choice is entirely one for you to make, and there is no correct answer. The luxury is in having the choice available to you.

Think backwards from the glowing future (think big!)

An obvious fact about any new business is that it is usually small. That is normal.

The problem is that the smallness of the business can promote *small thinking* among its founders. Small thinking is not expansive thinking. Small thinking will keep your business small by stymieing its natural growth potential. Excessive quantities of small thinking must therefore be avoided, even (especially!) in small businesses.

The type of small thinking that is relevant to this chapter is present-day-only thinking.

Present-day-only thinking is all about what your business needs are right now, in this moment. While you are busy doing hard work within the business, you are engaged in present-day-only thinking.

There is nothing wrong with thinking about current business needs. It is a vital part of running your business. But thinking *only* about present day issues will obscure your view of the future needs of your business.

Thinking backwards

The solution to this problem is thinking backwards from the future.

Thinking backwards from the future is about contemplating the actions that you will need to take in the present to achieve your business aspirations. Thinking backwards from the future is about ensuring that the actions that you take today will smooth the way for growth tomorrow. Thinking backwards from the future is about thinking big.

This type of thinking is expansive thinking. It can be the difference between future business success and being forever stuck in smallness.

A concern that entrepreneurs often express about this type of thinking relates to finance – they point out that the business is not currently able to afford costly measures. This concern is understandable.

In the present day, while you are frantically busy, future thinking appears to be an unaffordable luxury that frankly you don't have time for. However, expansive thinking does not have to lead to expensive measures. In other words, thinking from the future doesn't necessarily mean that your costs will increase in the present.

My first business was named after its first product. In those early days, I didn't realise that it was the 'first' product, since it was the *only* product. My thinking didn't go beyond doing what was necessary to make that product successful. After it did become successful, we wanted to introduce new products.

The problem was that we were stymied by both the company name and its website domain name, which were both the same name as the first product. Company names and domain names can be changed of course, but there are costs involved in making those changes. The cost may not be only in time and money, but also in reputation. Had I thought about the possible growth potential at the beginning, I would have chosen a domain name and company name which would allow for future unrestricted growth. There would have been no additional expense involved.

A similar error was made when we set up our first electronic invoicing system. Initially we used just four figures for the invoice number. In other words, we didn't foresee that we would, ever, issue more than 9,999 invoices! To have used a five or six digit numbering system at an early stage would have cost us no more money at that time. But to change the system later involved a cost.

Future vision

The best way to avoid small thinking is to have a vision for the future.

To do this, take some time to imagine what your business will look like when it's complete. Be clear in your mind about what your income will be, how many customers you will serve, and how you will feel at that future time.

Don't dwell on the steps that will be necessary to get there – the exact method does not matter at this stage. Remain flexible so that organic growth flows freely, and opportunities are not missed. And don't get too attached to the exact outcome either. It doesn't matter that your business won't eventually look exactly like the end result that you originally imagined. Instead, the objective of imagining and visualising the future is to install into your brain a sub-conscious image of how things might look in large scale.

> *"Imagination is more important than knowledge."*
> – ALBERT EINSTEIN

Creating this mental image (visualisation) of your future business will sub-consciously encourage you to take actions and decisions that are consistent with your goals for your business. It will also make your future success much more likely.

Whatever is created is first imagined.

Guilt – get over it

Hard work, for some entrepreneurs, is driven by guilt.

Guilt is debilitating. It is energy draining. And it causes ineffective decision-making.

Most people will do almost anything to avoid feeling guilty, including indulging in excessive working practices. Often the drive to avoid feelings of guilt is sub-conscious – we work hard to avoid feeling it, but we don't really know that we are doing this.

What do we feel guilty about?

The answer is pretty much everything. Humans seem to have an excessive need to guilt trip themselves. Let's take a look at some common examples for entrepreneurs.

Some business creators feel guilty about *not* working hard. The hard work ethic is, after all, prolific. Standard thinking dictates that proper success is achieved only by very hard work. These types of entrepreneurs use hard work to avoid feeling guilty for not working hard! The price that they pay is excessive work, and all its consequences.

Some entrepreneurs (especially those that suffer from low self esteem) feel guilty about taking time out for rest and relaxation. They think that they do not 'deserve' the downtime. These types of entrepreneurs maintain hard work in order to avoid the guilt associated with relaxation. This type of guilt can lead to illness.

Other entrepreneurs use hard work to avoid feeling guilty about something unrelated to work. For example, there may be events in the past which are too painful to think about, because of the way we acted, or because of a way that we feel we should have acted but didn't. For these types of entrepreneurs, hard work is an analgesic against the guilt that they would otherwise have *time* to feel. This is an insidious type of guilt that will lead to burnout unless it is dealt with.

Guilt is optional

The good news is that you don't *have* to feel guilty, ever.

The reality is that guilt is the end result of a particular way of thinking. And you can choose to think non-guilt-inducing thoughts instead.

Whoa, I hear you protest, surely guilt is an emotion rather than a way of thinking, and as human beings we have no choice but to feel an emotion. This is a point of view that is common, but is it correct? Let's take a closer look.

Why do we feel feelings of guilt? Isn't it because there is a thought that lies behind the guilt, which generates the guilty feeling?

For example, if you are an aspiring professional golfer, you might feel guilty about watching television, thinking that you should be spending time practising on the golf course instead. If you are an entrepreneur, you might feel guilty about playing golf, thinking that you should be in the office working hard instead. In both cases, first comes the thinking ("I should be playing golf", and "I should be in the office"), and it is that thinking that leads to the feeling of guilt.

Remove the thinking, and you remove the guilt.

Does guilt actually exist?

As the philosopher Friedrich Nietzsche said of the 18th century practice of killing women who were suspected of witchcraft, "*Although the most acute judges of the witches, and even the witches themselves, were convinced of the guilt of witchery, the guilt nevertheless was non-existent. It is thus with all guilt.*"

Nietzsche is saying that guilt does not exist in reality.

If guilt truly doesn't actually exist outside of our creating it with our thinking, then there is not much point in spending time on it. Working hard because of feelings of guilt would therefore seem inappropriate, to say the least.

Guilt is caused by wrong thinking

If we can agree that guilt is a waste of time and guilty thinking risks destruction of your business, then we could say that guilt is a feeling that is generated by wrong thinking. In this context, wrong thinking is thinking that doesn't serve you.

If you agree with me so far, then this means that any type of thinking which causes you to feel guilty is wrong thinking and needs to be dealt with.

Instead of doing wrong thinking, you need to *re-think* any thoughts that lead to feelings of guilt. This can be done by taking a careful look at the thoughts and making a different choice.

Getting rid of being guilt ridden

Despite the advice from Nietzsche, guilt can seem pretty darn real.

But since we know that guilt threatens the survival of our business, and consigns us to hard work, what can we do?

The answer is that you need to become aware of the guilt that you feel. Notice when you are feeling guilty and take a look at it. Say to yourself: "Oh look, I'm feeling guilty right now." Have a little laugh to yourself about the insanity of feeling something that doesn't exist, and move on. This might sound odd, and easier said than done. But it's actually not too hard. And practise makes it easier. It does require self-awareness, but that's a skill you need as an entrepreneur in any case.

If you think that the previous paragraph is a bit crazy, then try this solution instead: go to work on changing the context of the thinking on which the guilt is based.

For example, in the case of the entrepreneur who feels guilty about playing golf, a useful re-think would be: "It's actually fine for me to play golf because I find it relaxing, and I have great ideas when I am relaxed".

In this new way of thinking, the guilt does not get created because there is a new context which better serves the entrepreneur.

The new context is the benefits of the relaxation which derive from playing golf.

For several years I struggled with feelings of guilt associated with employing people. It seemed contradictory to me that, on the one hand, I was promoting a life of freedom for entrepreneurs (including myself). And on the other, I was employing people to do the work that I used to do. My freedom was purchased on the backs of others.

I discussed the guilty feelings with friends many times. Their caring counsel to me was always consistent: my business was providing well-paid jobs to people who were working in an enjoyable environment with generous vacation time. And yet the feelings of guilt remained.

Then one day I realised that not everyone is suited to being an entrepreneur. In that moment I suddenly appreciated that some people prefer the security of regular income and a stable job. The guilt immediately vanished. The context that created the guilt had changed. There was no space for the guilt in the new way of thinking. I was free of it.

What do you feel guilty about? How could a new perspective help you to banish your guilt?

Abolishing "should"

I'd like to see the word "should" abolished from the vocabulary of business creators.

What on earth could be wrong with "should", you may ask. Isn't it a vitally useful word for everyday communication? Wouldn't a person's ability to express themselves be restricted by its absence?

Far from it.

"Should" is a pernicious word that can be enormously destructive. It can get in the way of success by sapping the life energy of entrepreneurs. It can irretrievably separate you from your dreams and desires, leading to great unhappiness. It can single-handedly cause the death of your business.

The problem with "should"

Imagine for a moment that you are unsure about something. It could be a decision that you need to make, a type of business activity that you are considering, or even whether to continue on your entrepreneurial path.

How do you make the decision? More often than not, you will ask yourself: "What should I do?"

This is a question that you must never, ever, ask.

The problem with this question, and all similar uses of "should," is that it refers to a standard that is not your own. It represents an abdication of your personal power to think for yourself and to make your own decisions. It elevates the opinion of others above your own opinions. It creates a mental environment which is insecure and constantly questioning itself.

When people ask "what should I do", they are actually asking what others would want or expect them to do. What would my friends think? What would my parents want me to do? What is usual or common in society? Although the answers to these questions might be interesting in the abstract, they must never be used as the sole determinant for your own decisions.

> *"Think not of ... what [others]*
> *have done or not done.*
> *Think rather of ... the things*
> *you have done or not done."*
> – Buddha

Although there are many commonalities amongst us humans, each person is a unique expression of humanity. Our differences are reflected in the fact that no two people have the same fingerprints, the same iris pattern or the same bodily smell. Similarly, we all experience the world differently due to our unique filters through which we perceive the events that we witness. In the same way, no two people have precisely the same aspirations and goals. Your own understanding of the world and your desires for your life are unique to you.

Living your life according to "should" is therefore living your life mistakenly. Using "should" as your guide will never be fulfilling for *you*. In order to be truly satisfied you must do what *you* love to do, what *you* most desire, what *you* dream about doing when *you* are running wild with *your* imagination. It has nothing to do with what others think you should do.

Our addiction to "should" likely comes from a belief that in order to be liked by others, we must do what is expected of us. This is understandable – it is what we were taught as children. As a child, it's a useful starting place for determining a course of action. The problem is that most people continue to operate this way long into adult life.

The freedom entrepreneur never uses "should" to choose an action. Instead she asks herself, "What is the action that is most likely to achieve the desired result?"

"Should", on the other hand, is all about what is normal or what is expected.

What is generally expected of people is that they don't do anything too unusual, anything that rocks the boat, anything that focuses attention on them or their activities. This is unacceptable for the freedom entrepreneur. Because the freedom entrepreneur needs to operate outside the standard boundaries of behaviour, beyond the realm of what is usual and comfortable.

Take a look at the following statements. Do you agree that these are normal views that are held by most people? Then think about this: are they appropriate for you?

- I *should* work very hard to grow my business

- Only when my business is very profitable *should* I consider taking on staff

- Despite all my hard work, my business is not growing, so I *should* go back to my old job

- Given that so many people fail, I *shouldn't* have such silly ideas about becoming a successful entrepreneur

"Should" thinking is powerless thinking. It is powerless because it destroys your own freedom of choice. When you ask "what should I do?", you are actually asking "what do I think that others think that I should do?" Such a question is bordering on insanity, not least because we never really know what others are actually thinking.

I'm not saying that other people's advice is not valuable. It can be very useful. But asking for advice from people you trust, and taking into account that advice when deciding what is best for you, is very different from abdicating your personal power to think for yourself.

Following "should" as your guiding principle will eventually lead to resentment and frustration. It will instil within you an unnerving suspicion that you are living your life according to standards and values that have been set by others. It will lead to a lack of personal fulfilment and perhaps even despair. While original thought is the hallmark of the successful entrepreneur, "should" thinking discourages such risky pastimes.

How can you give up "should"?

My suggestion is that you go cold turkey. Just stop using the word.

Every time you hear yourself about to say "should", replace it with language that empowers you. For example, rather than ask, "what *should* I do?" ask "what *could* I do?" Can you hear the change in emphasis and meaning? Can you feel the power flowing back into your personal ability to choose?

The question "what *could* I do?" presupposes that you are able to judge for yourself what is best for you. And it opens up possibilities that were unavailable when your thinking was mired in the "should" mentality.

Living your life according to what you think other people think you should do is not the way of the freedom entrepreneur. If you would love to own a successful business while being personally free from hard work, then you will need to take the action that is consistent with that goal, irrespective of what other people think about it.

Remember that the majority of people never start down the entrepreneurial path, choosing instead to spend their working life as an employee. That may be right for them. But that doesn't mean that it's right for you.

Similarly most people believe that hard work should always be a prerequisite for entrepreneurial success. Do you still believe that?

Staying open (avoiding cynicism)

Part Two has been about developing flexibility in your thinking.

In addition to the specific topics discussed in this Part, it's important to generate and maintain a general openness to new opportunities and new methodologies for running your business. What I am asking here, is that you simply tune into 'possibility' once in a while. Don't close your mind to new ways of doing things.

If you find yourself dismissing a new idea out of hand, without really considering whether it might have any merit for you, then stop yourself. Think again. Allow yourself the opportunity to look at the idea to see how it might work. If you remain convinced that it's not appropriate for your business, that's fine. You can congratulate yourself on a job well done.

Being open to the new possibility is the key. It would be ridiculous to implement every new idea that is conveyed to you. But once in a while there will be something that comes along that will be useful, and which you will choose to implement with great success.

An important feature of maintaining an open mind is that it will prevent you from becoming cynical. Cynicism is the refuge of the disappointed, the disaffected, the disillusioned, the disenchanted and the dissatisfied.

A pervasive attitude of cynicism prevents us being open to new ideas, including new ways of working and new ways to serve our customers. Remember that if you are not open to 'better', you will most definitely attract more of the same.

The freedom entrepreneur guards herself against cynicism, and remains open to possibilities.

Part Three

Preparing for Freedom

*"The revelation of thought takes men
out of servitude into freedom."*
– RALPH WALDO EMERSON

Why freedom is vital

The key message of the book is that massive business success is entirely achievable without hard work. In fact, I'd like to venture further: hard work will usually lead to business failure.

Parts One and Two therefore looked at why hard work must be avoided, and how to go about changing the foundations of thinking that cause us to fall into the trap of hard work.

Part Three looks at the vitally important flip side of the same coin: why your own freedom is an essential ingredient for your journey into business success, and how to go about achieving it.

Because if you don't achieve freedom from hard work, the best outcome is that your business will continue to grow slowly, while you work harder and harder. A less satisfactory outcome is that you will go into burnout, which may lead to the end of your business aspirations. Neither of these options is attractive. And neither is necessary.

What I am suggesting, as an alternative, is that you work less. Very much less. And at the same time that you are working very much less, your business will grow rapidly and become much more profitable.

So this must now be your focus: less work and more profitability.

It's not only possible, it's entirely achievable. However, before we can get there, we need to take a look at an important problem.

The problem is this: since you are currently doing hard work, we can be certain that your current way of operating is not appropriately aligned for future success. In fact, your current way of working is fundamentally flawed. It is the same flaw that exists in most small businesses.

That flaw is hard work (and lack of freedom).

So, we are going to make some alterations to the foundations of your business and to the way that you work. The main objective of these alterations is to create freedom time for you, so that you can become the freedom entrepreneur, as opposed to the hard working entrepreneur.

In order to make these foundational changes, you must go back to the beginning of your entrepreneurial journey. You must re-create your business from the ground up, so as to reduce your personal role within it. You must reinvent your business so that it is able to function without you.

Yes, you did read that correctly: your business must be able to function without you! What I mean by this is that your constant attention must not be a pre-requisite to the day-to-day operation of the business.

Before you accuse me of losing track of reality (and you request that I jump off the nearest bridge) please be reassured that I'm not saying that you must not be *involved* in your business. I'm saying that the proper functioning of your business must not *depend* on you. It is critical that you understand that you will not be able to grow your business effectively unless you are free from doing everything that needs to be done within the business.

> *"Freedom is nothing but a chance to be better."*
> – ALBERT CAMUS

Just in case you need further persuasion, the aspiration of rapid and effective business growth is not the only reason to give up hard work. Take a look at the following points, and see if you agree with them:

- If you are constantly needed within your business in order for it to function, then it's not your business – it's your job. You don't want another job. Giving up a job was one of the reasons that you became an entrepreneur.

- In order to be a valuable asset (whether or not you intend to sell it) your business must be able to operate without you. No one will want to buy your business – and therefore it will have little value – if you are personally essential to its day-to-day operations. Another way of saying this is that the less you are needed, the more valuable your business will be.

- Assuming that you are even vaguely sane, you will not want to be working all of your awake time in the future. You will want the freedom to enjoy the fruits of your labour – to relax, to enjoy being with your family and friends, to do what you love to do, and perhaps to start and grow new businesses.

For these reasons, as well as all the ones that we looked at in Part One, your goal must now be to create freedom from hard work. But what does freedom from hard work actually mean, and what would it look like for you? These are questions that business creators rarely consider – they are so busy working that they cannot even imagine how it could be any different.

> *"Everything that is really great and inspiring*
> *is created by the individual*
> *who can labour in freedom."*
> – ALBERT EINSTEIN

To put it very simply, freedom from hard work means that you no longer do *any* hard work. This doesn't mean that you no longer work. What it means is that the work that you do will be very different in type and quantity from the work that you did when you were working hard.

Right now you are most likely doing all or most of the day-to-day tasks that comprise the nuts and bolts of the business operations. The objective is for you to stop this completely. You will achieve this result incrementally, over a relatively short period of time.

The end result of these changes will be that you will become the freedom entrepreneur.

To put it another way, your time in the very near future will be spent working *on* your business, rather than *in* your business. This is the single most important concept in the book. Working *on* your business is the role of the freedom entrepreneur. Working *in* your business is an activity that you will no longer engage in.

What does it mean to work *in* the business?

Working in the business is performing tasks that comprise the role of a *producer*.

The work of a producer (production work) is typically the work that is carried out by an employee or someone who is self-employed. Production work, in the context of small businesses (as opposed to filming movies), is all the stuff that is directly involved with producing the product or service that your business sells. It's the coalface work.

In a hair salon, production work is cutting hair, ordering and sorting supplies, cleaning equipment and floors, and taking payments from customers for the service.

In the hotel trade, production work is taking bookings, welcoming guests, ordering supplies, cooking and serving food, cleaning rooms, and maintaining the building.

In a law firm, production work includes marketing the firm's services, providing legal advice, and producing and sending invoices.

There is nothing wrong with production work. It's absolutely vital that production work gets done. But production work is not the work of the freedom entrepreneur.

The freedom entrepreneur works *on* the business

In order to achieve the freedom time that is necessary for fast and effective business growth, you must drastically reduce your role as producer. The amount of freedom that you enjoy in the future will be directly proportionate to how successful you are right now in setting up the business to function, mostly, without you.

Remember the chart from Part One? Here it is again, including the distinctions between working *in* your business and working *on* your business.

Time Spent in a Typical Day

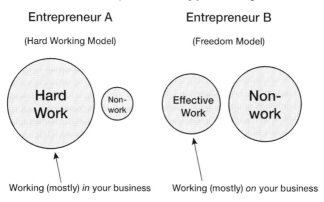

Entrepreneur A

(Hard Working Model)

Entrepreneur B

(Freedom Model)

Hard Work

Non-work

Effective Work

Non-work

Working (mostly) *in* your business   Working (mostly) *on* your business

This Part of the book looks at the foundational steps that are needed so that your business can evolve into a well-functioning automated machine for producing what you want, including your own personal freedom and wealth. These steps constitute working on the business, rather than in the business. Working only on the business will become your most important task going forward.

Introducing the freedom machine

Creating the freedom machine is the whole purpose of this book.

The freedom machine is your business, restructured. It's your business producing exactly what it produces now, but in an entirely different way. It's your ticket to much less work and much more business growth.

Building the freedom machine is therefore the work of the freedom entrepreneur. Nothing is as important to the success of your business as the work you do in creating the freedom machine. All of the effort that you expend in order to bring about the birth of the freedom machine is entrepreneurial work, rather than production work.

> *"Our freedom can be measured*
> *by the number of things*
> *that we can walk away from."*
> – VERNON HOWARD

The freedom machine is a re-engineered version of your business. The re-engineered version does not depend on you for its functioning. Instead, it is a well-maintained and automated money-making engine, designed primarily for the fulfilment of your desires. It is an asset that produces wealth, with very little input from you.

So your objective, your vitally urgent task from this moment forward, is to convert your business into the freedom machine. Before you can do this, you need to:

- Understand how your business works

- Prepare to offload some of your current workload

- Create and implement business procedures

- Become an effective leader and delegator

These topics are handled in the remainder of the book. Before we get into them, we need to look at an important distinction between two different, and geometrically opposed, types of entrepreneurial behaviour: being reactive and being proactive.

Reactive versus proactive

Understanding the difference between reactivity and proactivity is an essential prerequisite for achieving freedom and rapid business growth.

Being *reactive* is the hallmark of the overly busy entrepreneur, the self-employed person and the ambitious employee. Being *proactive* is the signature of the freedom entrepreneur.

Right now, your working day is likely characterised by a preponderance of reactivity. In order to get you out of your reactive habit, we need to make a radical change in your working practices. We need to move you from being primarily reactive to being primarily proactive.

Being reactive

When you are reactive, you are essentially in the state of being responsive to events. Something happens, and you do something as a result.

While this way of working may seem entirely normal, it will not lead to business success. Take a look at the following examples of reactive behaviour:

- An order comes in to your business … and you do what must be done to handle the order

- A phone call is made to your business regarding a query about your products … and you take the call and deal with what needs to be done to handle the query

- A problem arises with a customer … and you take the necessary steps to sort out the issue

- A client requests a service to be performed … and you provide the service to the client

If this looks very much like your own way of working, your day is mostly about reacting to what happens. In one sense, your behaviour is entirely appropriate. In another sense, you are completely out of control. The reason that you are completely out of control is because your working day is about dancing to the tune of other people's agendas. What we want instead is for your day to be self-governed.

It is not possible to become the freedom entrepreneur (which requires you to create your own freedom machine) while you are primarily in reactive mode. Therefore, before you can become the freedom entrepreneur, you must extricate yourself from being at the mercy of events and move into a state in which you are the creator of events.

Being proactive

Being proactive is being in a state of grounded control. It is about calmly and deliberately implementing the items on your agenda.

In proactive mode, you determine how things are going to be, and you take steps to bring about those things. Being proactive means being free from distraction – as soon as you are distracted from the task in hand, you have become reactive. You cannot be proactive and reactive at the same time.

Don't panic, I'm not asking you to be proactive *all* of the time! There will inevitably be occasions when, even as the freedom entrepreneur, you will need to be reactive. For example, you will need to take account of what others are doing and, initially at least, handle emergencies when they arise.

But you must now start to increase the proportion of your day that you are creating events, and reduce the proportion of your day that has events governing you.

How do you become more proactive?

Becoming more proactive is about developing conscious awareness. It requires you to take a look at your standard working day, to identify the circumstances where you tend to be reactive, and to remove that reactivity from your behaviour.

You can do this by making two key changes.

The first change involves taking a look at your automatic reactions. Automatic reactions are spontaneous behaviours which arise on the occurrence of specific events. For example, Sarah hears the beep of an incoming message on her phone, and she immediately goes to take a look.

To remove automatic reactions from your daily work, you first need to identify them. Make a list of the things that happen which cause you to react automatically.

Then, when those things next happen, either do *nothing* or do something *other* than what you would have done before.

Not responding automatically to events takes a great deal of self-awareness and self-control. Initially it may be highly uncomfortable for you to do something other than you customarily would have done. And it may seem illogical or even counterproductive. Do it anyway. The point here is not to cause chaos for yourself, but rather to give yourself the opportunity to practise being in control of your day.

The second change requires you to take steps that will reduce the *quantity* of events to which you will need to react. For example, Ben is working on a plan to create his freedom machine when he notices incoming emails. He immediately switches to his email programme so that he can read the messages. In doing so he has become distracted from the task at hand.

Making this second change again requires self-awareness. You need to take a look at your working day and make a list of the things that occur that will cause you to be distracted. Then, take actions that prevent those things from happening.

What action could Ben take to remove the possibility of being distracted by arriving emails? One answer is that he could turn off the automatic send/receive function in his email programme. If this idea causes you to turn blue with fright, don't panic! You can still manually choose to receive emails when you are ready.

The important thing is that you will have temporarily removed the distraction of incoming emails when you are engaged with other tasks.

After removing your automatic reactions and reducing the frequency of events that cause you to react, you will notice that your working day will begin to feel different. You will have more time, you will be more focussed and you will feel in greater control. These are the attributes of the freedom entrepreneur.

Urgent versus important

As a frantically busy entrepreneur, it's very likely that you spend most of your day handling emergencies.

In fact, you are probably so busy handling emergencies that you have little time to do anything else. You are stressed out, and everything that happens must be taken care of immediately. You spend most of your day fighting fires, and almost no time investing in your future freedom.

We are going to work on ditching this self-destructive behaviour. Instead, you are going to set priorities.

Setting priorities is about changing the order in which you do things. To understand the change that is needed, we need to make a distinction between two types of task: things that are urgent, and things that are important.

Right now, in reactive mode, you handle the urgent things first. That's normal and usual, for employees and hard working entrepreneurs. But that way of working will not allow you to become the freedom entrepreneur. Instead, you need to stop doing what's urgent, and start doing what's important.

In other words, you need to do the *important things first*, and tackle the urgent stuff only *after* the important work is complete. Although this may sound entirely counterintuitive, or at least bizarrely unreasonable, this change in your daily working practice is essential. Only by making this change will it become possible for you to build the freedom machine.

So let's take a look at the distinction between urgent things and important things.

What are the urgent things?

The urgent things are all the jobs that seem like they have to be done immediately. It's the stuff that is screaming for your attention.

Examples include overdue reminders for bills that need to be paid, complaints from customers that need to be handled, queries about your business's products and services that need to be answered, orders that need to be fulfilled, repairs to equipment that need to be made, and raw materials that need to be purchased.

The urgent stuff is almost always producer work (working *in* your business). Producer work is not the work of the freedom entrepreneur.

What are the important things?

The important things are all the tasks that are involved in building the freedom machine (in other words, everything that the book is asking you to do). Nothing is as important to the future success of your business as these tasks.

Important stuff and urgent stuff are not the same things. Since you can't do both the urgent stuff and the important stuff in any one moment, you have to make a choice.

Choosing to prioritise building the freedom machine is the choice of the freedom entrepreneur. It is about investment in your future free self. It can be challenging to put aside the urgent stuff, but it must be done.

How do you prioritise the important things?

The first thing you must acknowledge, and become comfortable with, is that the urgent stuff must fall by the wayside.

There is no getting around this obvious fact. It's very scary. And your business may suffer a drop in income during this critical phase of change. You will need to have faith that the reduction will be temporary. And remember that doing the important things now will result in there being far fewer urgent things for you to do in the future.

The best way to prioritise the important things is to make a list each morning of the tasks that you need to complete that day.

The tasks on your list will all be important ones, none of them urgent.

Ensure that you complete the tasks on your list for the day. Do your best not to get distracted. If you do get lost in other things – including reacting to events and handling emergencies – don't panic! Instead, complete the stuff that you feel you have to do, and then return to your list of important things. If you don't get all the important things completed that day, copy the remaining ones to your list for the next working day.

The remainder of the book describes the important things that you will need to get done in order to achieve freedom. Before we can find out exactly what they are for *your* business, we first need to ensure that you understand how your business currently works.

Understanding your business

Right now your business works only because you do.

Your business functions only because you personally do most everything that has to be done to make it function. This means that the way that the business currently works is all about you. Without you, everything would fall apart. Because if you are not there, all the vital jobs that need to get done won't get done. Let's call this the standard model for running a small business.

The problem with the standard model is that it's not sustainable. And, it's not scalable. This type of working will lead to burnout. Because as the business grows, your workload will also grow.

So a new model is needed.

The new model is the model of the freedom entrepreneur. To morph from the standard model to the freedom model requires radical action. The action that is needed is what this book is all about.

It starts with you learning about how your business actually works.

Because it's very likely that you don't know how your business works. You don't know how your business works because you've never taken the time to think about it. This is not a criticism. And it's not your fault. It's just a fact – you are busy. But until you know how your business works, you won't properly understand how to grow it. You won't know which bits of what you currently do could be given to someone else to do. And, most importantly, you will be unable to convert your business into the freedom machine.

The truth is that right now your business doesn't work – *you* do!

So now it's time for you to get very clear about how your business functions. It's time to get organised.

In order to get organised, you are going to create a diagram. The diagram will show your business in a way that you may not have previously thought about. It will be a graphic representation of the operating structure of your business, as it is right now – an overview of what actually happens in your business on a daily basis.

There is a key difference between this diagram and traditional organisational diagrams. The difference is that this diagram is based on roles, not on people. This diagram will be a reflection of how your business looks right now in terms of the types of work that are actually being done.

At the current time, it may be that you do *everything* within the business. Or you may have a business partner or an employee who performs some of the roles. Either way, each of the *roles* will appear in the diagram.

To illustrate this type of diagram, I'd like to introduce you to Naomi.

Naomi's business

A couple of years ago Naomi quit her job as a manager of buildings in the public sector and started her own business. Her business provides management and refurbishment services to private landlords. She has one client who occupies the majority of her time. Her client buys residential properties that are in poor condition in order to refurbish them and then rent them out.

Naomi sources potential properties for her client to purchase by scouring advertisements from local real estate agents. Once her client has bought a property, she manages the refurbishment process. She assesses the work that needs to be done and then engages builders, plumbers, electricians, decorators and other trades people. When the work has been completed to a standard that she is happy with, she sets about furnishing the property.

At that point, the property is ready to be viewed by potential tenants, a process which she also manages. When a new tenant has been arranged, Naomi handles the moving-in process, including meeting the tenant at the property, dealing with the inventory checklist and handing over the keys.

For her work, Naomi charges a daily rate. She is highly motivated and very conscientious. She always wants to do the best job possible. Recently the quantity of work has started to mount up, and she finds that she is now working seven days a week, as well as many evenings.

By some measures Naomi is successful. She has started a business which makes money, and her services are obviously appreciated by her client. Although she has recently taken on a part-time personal assistant (Lily) to answer her business phone and keep an eye on her business email account, it is clear that she cannot go on indefinitely putting in the number of hours that she is currently working. Nor can she realistically expand the business using the current business model, which is that Naomi herself does almost all of the work that needs to be done.

Let's take a look at the diagram on page 94, which depicts the various roles in Naomi's business. We will refer to this as Naomi's Current Roles Diagram.

The first thing to notice about this diagram is that it is centred on roles. Each of the activities within Naomi's business is described separately in its own box. Each role-box also contains the name of the person who currently performs that role.

By taking a quick look at this diagram we can see that Naomi is doing almost everything in the business herself. The only work carried out by others is answering the telephone, handling emails and the tasks that are undertaken by the trades people.

This graphic representation of the roles within Naomi's business gives us insight into how Naomi's business actually works because it divides up her business into neat packages of activity. Looking at her Current Roles Diagram allows Naomi to view her business in a new way. She can now see a visual representation of the overall structure of her business.

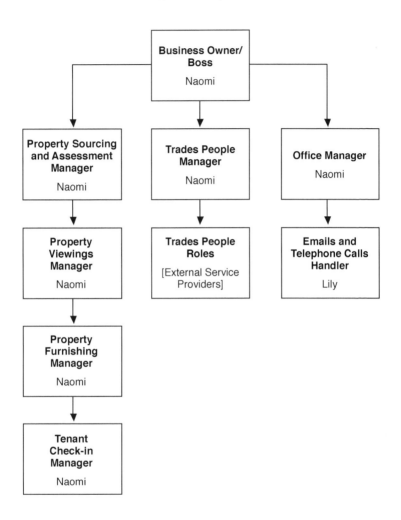

Creating your Current Roles Diagram

So, now it's time to create your own Current Roles Diagram.

On a piece of paper, make a list of all the roles within your business. Take some time to think carefully about everything that is done in the business, and make sure that you don't leave anything out. It's fine to include several items together under one heading, providing that the heading adequately covers all the items.

Then, create a structure of boxes similar to Naomi's diagram. Your own diagram will not necessarily look exactly like Naomi's diagram – that is fine because all businesses are different. However, there will likely be common elements between your own diagram and the diagram for Naomi's business (looking at other peoples' businesses, such as Naomi's, can be helpful in order to see if your business is missing one or more vital roles – more about this in the next chapter).

Once you have created the box structure, add a name against each of the roles in all of the boxes. This is the name of the person who currently performs the role. Most, or all, of the roles may be currently fulfilled by you. That is fine for now.

Take a look at your diagram. Hopefully it will enable you to get clearer about what you actually do on a daily basis. And you will see how the roles and tasks within the business fit with each other. Most importantly, you will be able to see which aspects of your current activities you can start to delegate.

Keep your diagram safe – you will need it later.

Producer versus entrepreneur

You now need to take a closer look at your standard working day.

You need to get a very clear understanding of the types of work that you are currently doing. In order to do this, we are going to divide your daily working activities into production work (working *in* the business) on the one hand, and entrepreneurial work (working *on* the business), on the other hand.

For your next working day, you are going to make a list of each task that you perform. Start from the moment you begin work, and finish at the end of your working day. As you complete each task, take a pause and make a note of the amount of time that you spent on that task.

Make sure you include on the list everything that you do in the day.

The object of making this list is not to make a judgement about the rightness or wrongness of what you are doing, but (for now) simply to include everything that you do.

At the end of the day, go back over the list and, for each task, write down whether it's production work or entrepreneurial work.

As a reminder of the distinction between these two types of work, production work is all the stuff that must be done in order to create or deliver the products or services that are sold by your business.

In a dentistry business, production work includes ordering supplies, cleaning equipment, mixing amalgam, drilling holes in teeth, affixing braces, cleaning teeth, fitting dentures and handling payments. In a tile manufacturing business, production work includes obtaining raw materials, mixing the materials, producing tiles, maintaining equipment, advertising the tiles, cleaning the store or warehouse, managing payments, handling complaints and dealing with refunds.

Entrepreneurial work, on the other hand, includes everything you do to bring about the birth of the freedom machine, taking key business decisions and managing growth opportunities.

The important thing for your list is that you have to choose one or the other – either production work or entrepreneurial work – for each task. If a task appears to be both (it can't be both), then sub-divide it into the parts of the task that you think are production work, and the parts that you think are entrepreneurial work. If you are unsure which one it is, then list it as production work.

The structure of your list could look something like the following table:

Task	Time	Production / Entrepreneurial

Once you have completed the table for your day's work, calculate how much time you spent working *in* the business (production work), and how much time you were working *on* the business (entrepreneurial work).

Below is an example of a completed task list. It shows that the entrepreneur spent 10 hours working, of which 9 hours was spent on production work. This ratio of production work to entrepreneurial work is common for most entrepreneurs. Of the total time worked, 90% was on production work, and 10% on entrepreneurial work.

Task	Time	Production / Entrepreneurial
Communicating with suppliers and placing orders for supplies	1½ hours	P
Contacting a customer regarding her query	½ hour	P
Thinking about a possible new product	½ hour	E
Proofreading marketing materials	2 hours	P
Tweaking the content of the website	2½ hours	P
Speaking with a customer about an order	½ hour	P
Placing an online advertisement for a new part time member of staff	½ hour	E
Sending invoices to customers	1 hour	P
Paying bills	1 hour	P

Total Time – 10 hours

Production Work – 9 hours

Entrepreneurial Work – 1 hour

Percentage of time on production work – 90%

How did you get on with your list? If the percentage of your time spent on production work is less than 90%, then you are already ahead of the game.

Two goals

As you continue to progress toward freedom entrepreneurship, you have two goals. The first goal is to steadily *increase* the proportion of your work time spent on entrepreneurial work. The second goal is to progressively *decrease* your total working time.

Right now you might be spending 100% of your time on production work. Don't panic. The point of the exercise is not to cause concern, but rather to give you insight into the type of work that you are doing. Now that you are better aware of the distinction between the amount of time you spend on production work and the amount of time you spend on entrepreneurial work, you will be surprised at how quickly your own working day will start to change.

Before you set aside the list that you created for today, put today's date at the top. Then for the next five working days, make a similar daily list. Keep the lists somewhere safe, as we will refer to them every so often.

And by the way, the time that you spend making the lists is time spent doing entrepreneurial work!

Your business re-engineered

So far in Part Three, you have been working on gathering the information that you need to start work on converting your business into the freedom machine.

You now know how your business actually works. You have identified the roles within the business. And you have become aware of the type of work that you spend your time doing (if you are a hard working entrepreneur, it's highly likely that the type of work you are doing is mostly reactive work and production work).

There are two more investigations that you need to make before you can embark on increasing your personal freedom and growing your business. The first is to discover which pieces of work you currently do that can be given to someone else to do. The second is to find out what other things will need to be done within the business to ensure its long-term prosperity.

To make these investigations, you are going to create a new roles diagram. This roles diagram will be based in the near future. It's up to you exactly what point in time this will be, although it's useful to work on a time frame of two years or less. The Future Roles Diagram is a depiction of your business at that future time.

Looking into the future

The Future Roles Diagram represents the culmination of your achievements in morphing yourself from production work into freedom entrepreneurialism. It therefore shows your business functioning as the freedom machine.

In order to produce the Future Roles Diagram, you will need to think about the changes that will need to have occurred between now and two years (or whatever time period you selected) from now.

In other words you must imagine yourself as the freedom entrepreneur two years into the future. Imagine how your business looks at that future time. And imagine how your own working day will look. You are no longer doing production work. And you have much more free time.

Then ask yourself the following question:

Standing two years in the future, and looking back at the current time, what changes would I have needed to have made during that two-year period?

This question requires you to imagine your future successful self. At that time you will be doing mostly entrepreneurial work (as opposed to production work). And you will have much more freedom time than you do today. Think about how your life, and your business, will look at that time. Then, keeping your mind on your future self, look back at yourself today (your hard working self), and make a list of the changes that would have needed to have been made between today and that future time.

It's not necessary, at this stage, to be concerned about *how* these changes will be implemented. All that you need to do is to be conscious of what those changes are.

For your list, you can just look at the big stuff. For example, you might have needed a bigger office, more employees, a larger customer base, a new supplier (or a larger number of suppliers), an office in another location or overseas. Keep the list of changes nearby, as you will need it very soon.

Back to the present

Now, take out your Current Roles Diagram and a blank piece of paper. For each one of the roles shown in the Current Roles Diagram that is currently *performed by you*, ask yourself the following two questions:

- Is the work comprised within that role a *necessary* part of the business?

- Could the tasks comprising the role be handled *other than by you*?

Let's take a closer look at how these two questions help you to create your Future Roles Diagram.

For the first question, if all or part of the work comprising the role is not necessary to the success of the business, then you can exclude the work when you are creating the Future Roles Diagram.

Work that is not necessary includes anything that is not needed for the long-term prosperity of the business. Only you know what you currently do that's not actually needed. Every entrepreneur does superfluous stuff – sometimes out of habit, sometimes out of superstition, sometimes because they just don't think about what's needed and what isn't.

So, take some time to exclude from your working practices all the non-needed stuff.

The second question requires you to think about the things that you currently do that you, *personally*, don't need to do. These are the things that still need to get done in the business, but which don't need to be done by *you*. It's the stuff that you currently do which could either be automated or which could be given to someone else to do. There is no need, at this stage, to figure out who is going to do the work – you just need to ascertain the things that don't need to be done by you.

As far as automation is concerned, this includes not only software-based solutions but also taking appropriate shortcuts. Many entrepreneurs, especially very busy ones, re-do work that they have done before, over and over. They are too stressed to even think about doing anything else, such as creating standard email templates or developing a 'frequently asked questions' page for their website.

When you are contemplating offloading some of your workload onto others, bear in mind that it can be very tempting to believe that it is *only you* who can possibly do some of the things that you currently do. You are requested to take a careful look at the reality of this belief. If the work is production work, then it is virtually certain that you don't personally need to do it.

The assumption that we are the only person on Planet Earth who can do a particular task is one of the reasons for the proliferation of hard work. More on this in Part Six.

Your Future Roles Diagram

Now it's time to create your Future Roles Diagram.

For each role, draw a box and add the name of the role. Then, for each box that contains a role which consists of production work, add a name other than your own to that box. If you don't have anyone in mind, that's fine for now – make up a name or use 'X'.

Next, take a look at a few (at least three) of your most recent daily lists of tasks. Make a double check that all of the necessary roles in the daily tasks lists are included somewhere in the Future Roles Diagram. If they are not, then add them in. If the roles consist of production work, remember to assign them to someone else (or use 'X').

Now that you have assigned all of the production work elsewhere, there is one more thing to think about. In order to function efficiently in the future, the freedom machine must be whole and complete. In other words it must contain all of the ingredients of a properly functioning business. It won't work properly otherwise.

A car can run quite well, for a period of time, without an air filter or without windscreen wipers. But eventually those missing bits will start to cause problems. It's the same with your business. It must have all necessary parts in order to function effectively in the longer term, especially if your freedom is to be guaranteed.

So take a look at the Future Roles Diagram that you have

created so far, and think about what else needs to be included. All additional items that need to be added will fall into one of two categories.

The first category consists of all the things which are currently important, but which are right now being neglected in your business. Each business is different, and therefore each business must be looked at separately to see what might be missing. Having said that, entrepreneurs (especially busy ones) often neglect at least one of the following major role types:

- Record keeping – keeping accurate business records, especially of financial transactions

- Accounts receivable – checking that customers are paying on time, and following-up if they don't

- Accounts payable – managing the function of paying suppliers

- Marketing – informing potential customers about the goods and services that your business sells

- Monitoring the competition – keeping an eye on what your competitors are doing, so that you can assess whether changes need to be made in your business

- Researching technological changes – staying up to date, especially as regards techniques and systems that can be used to automate your business processes

The second category consists of any new roles that are specific to your business that will become necessary when your business is much bigger than it is today. These additional roles are aspects of the future business which will be vital, but which you may currently be devoting very little time to. What these additional roles are for your business depends on the type of business you run.

So you must take some time to think about what your business will need in the near future in order to function as a well-oiled machine for the fulfilment of your needs, without you actually having to be present. Ask yourself what extra things will need to be done in the business so that it functions as the freedom machine.

Back to Naomi

Let's take another look at Naomi's Current Roles Diagram. Thinking about what else might need to be done within her business, we can see that there are two obvious roles that are missing:

• Financial record keeping

• Marketing

This is a valuable warning sign for Naomi that some changes need to be made straight away.

If no work is being done on preparing financial statements now, then there is a problem waiting to be discovered when it's time to file them and pay tax.

If marketing is being neglected now, then Naomi's business will be in big trouble if she loses her main client. And even if she retains her client, she cannot expect to acquire additional clients for the business if no marketing is being done.

Naomi's Future Roles Diagram

Let's say that we have now asked Naomi to create her Future Roles Diagram.

To do this, she has imagined her business two years into the future. By that future time, she would have established an on-line presence to help with promotion and marketing. She would have engaged people to carry out the day-to-day production roles within the business. She would have established roles for accounts management. And her own role would have morphed from producer into CEO.

Here is the Future Roles Diagram that Naomi produced:

NAOMI'S FUTURE ROLES DIAGRAM (TWO YEARS AHEAD)

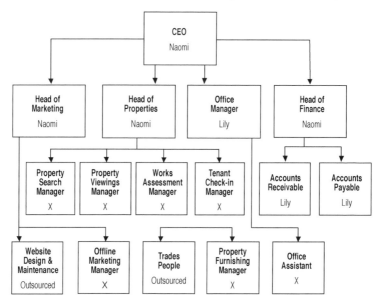

From Naomi's Future Roles Diagram, we can see that she has been thinking big! There are several additional roles established, and she has clearly envisaged the business doing significantly more work than it does today.

Naomi has placed herself in the position of CEO.

Although she has retained a managerial role in many of the activities of the business (she will not be as free as would be ideal two years into the future), she has delegated much of the production work that goes on in those roles.

She has obviously thought about marketing, since the future business has a Marketing Manager (which may initially be a part-time role). Naomi has created a new position of Head of Finance (which she fills) and has increased Lily's roles to include Accounts Receivable (handling invoices that the business sends to its clients) and Accounts Payable (handling bills that the business needs to pay to its suppliers).

Although there are further roles that Naomi could delegate, her Future Roles Diagram shows that she is well on her way to creating the freedom machine.

What you now know

The information that you have gathered as a result of your work in this Part is vital preparatory work for building your freedom machine.

Importantly, two things will have become clear to you:

• The areas of your business which are currently being neglected

• The tasks that you can delegate right now so that your time is freed up to work on building the freedom machine

Next, take out your Current Roles Diagram and place it next to your Future Roles Diagram. You will now clearly see:

• Where you are right now

• Where you are destined to be in the near future

Making a comparison between the two diagrams reveals the work that needs to get done between now and then in order to bring about the new reality. This is the work of the freedom entrepreneur.

One thing that will become entirely obvious (if it hasn't already) is that you will need other people to help you create the freedom machine.

Part Four

Getting Beyond Yourself

"Ask not what your teammates can do for you.
Ask what you can do for your teammates."
– MAGIC JOHNSON

Why you must look beyond yourself

Creating and sustaining a successful enterprise is not a solo job.

Entrepreneurs who work alone could be described as being 'self-employed'. There is nothing wrong with being self-employed. Being self-employed brings many advantages over being an employee. But being self-employed will not lead to significant financial wealth and freedom from hard work.

If you are to acquire both freedom and financial independence, you must involve other people in your entrepreneurial journey. Remember that our goal is for the profitability of your business to grow rapidly, and for your personal freedom to increase significantly. You cannot achieve this on your own. You are going to need help.

The problem is that business creators are often highly resistant to getting (and asking for) help. Why is this?

At the beginning of their entrepreneurial journey, business creators have a deep desire to 'go it alone'. This is not surprising since, in most cases, they were working for someone else at the time that they decided to set up a business. They wanted to escape the daily routine. They wanted respite from being told what to do. They wanted to directly benefit from the hard work and long hours that they were putting in. They wanted to be in charge of their own destiny.

Being in charge of your own destiny implies noble and lofty aspirations of overcoming challenges and achieving goals, without needing anyone's help to do it.

The problem is that this way of thinking is flawed. Because although the lone warrior attitude is often essential to inspire and motivate entrepreneurs to *commence* a business, it is not helpful when it comes to *growing* the business. And it certainly won't facilitate your personal freedom.

Asking for help is scary

Solo entrepreneurs frequently find the idea of taking on someone to help them a deeply unsettling one. The reason for this is usually that they have one or more of the following beliefs:

- It's impossible to choose the right person

- People are just out for what they can get

- Employees are a waste of time and resources

- Being responsible for another person is too challenging

- Employees are too expensive

- An employee would not know what to do in the business

- Mistakes on the job mean that employees are more trouble than they are worth

- No one but me can do the job

As long as these beliefs are stronger than the desire to do what it takes to succeed, hard work will always be the result. What it actually takes, to win the game of creating a growing business while securing your own personal freedom, is the involvement of other people.

Things must change

Right now you are working too many hours. You have been doing so for far too long. And if you keep up your current workload, you will soon have no life outside of your business.

What we want instead is for your business to grow quickly, and at the same time for you to work less. These two goals are not incompatible. But in order to get there we need to take a clear and honest look at the situation.

If your business is to become much more profitable than it is right now, then one (or preferably both) of the following two things must occur:

- The number of customers must increase
- The existing customers must be served more

There is no getting around this. And it's obvious that each of these outcomes will take time and effort to achieve. Who is going to do the extra work that is required? You? I don't think so. You are already working much too hard. If not you, then we need to look elsewhere.

Here is the truth: you cannot effectively grow your business without help.

The help is going to be provided by other people. The reticence that entrepreneurs experience when they contemplate seeking help can be overcome by understanding the benefits.

Having people around you to share the journey of business creation and growth is essential. Not just because it frees you from hard work. Here is an unwritten rule of the universe: two people working on a common goal can achieve far more than two people working alone on separate goals. With three people working together, there is another exponential jump in what becomes achievable.

It is one of the 'laws' of business that it takes more than one person to accomplish almost everything that is worthwhile.

The leverage of others

The benefit of working with others is not merely a disproportionate increase in what becomes possible. By utilising the services and skills of other people, your business will effectively be leveraging their time. In other words, the rise in productivity will be accompanied by a rise in both business activity and profit.

Here is something that it's critical to understand: the amount of extra income per additional person working in your business will usually be significantly more than it costs to hire or engage that person.

To put it another way, almost all business growth is people dependent. Essentially, you cannot afford *not* to take on people to help you.

Naomi again

Let's revisit Naomi's business, and take a closer look at her financial situation.

As we know from Naomi's Current Roles Diagram, she was working mostly alone (with a bit of help from Lily). Working at her maximum capacity – all day and most evenings, seven days a week – she completed work on one new apartment every month. The net income (profit) was £5,000 per apartment.

So Naomi's business was making £60,000 (£5,000 x 12) per year in profit.

When she saw the differences between her Current Roles Diagram and her Future Roles Diagram, Naomi decided to take on a part-time assistant. The assistant did some of the tasks that Naomi used to do – furnishing the properties, handling the viewings, and managing tenant check-ins.

This meant that Naomi became free for two full days per week.

For part of her newly acquired free time, Naomi worked on getting new clients for the business. For the remainder, she relaxed and visited friends. Soon after making this change, she was successful in getting two new clients. So she took on an additional part-time assistant to handle the extra work.

By this stage, her business was completing three apartments per month. The monthly income was therefore £15,000 (£5,000 x 3). So the yearly income had grown from £60,000 to £180,000.

The two assistants cost the business a total of £3,000 per month (£36,000 per year), leaving a net income of £12,000 per month (£15,000 – £3,000).

So Naomi's business was now making £144,000 per year (£12,000 x 12) in profit.

Naomi could not have achieved this growth in income and profitability (and the increase in personal freedom) without taking on help.

You are different? Really?

"But," I hear you say, "in my case it's different."

Let me stop you there. I think that you are about to say that *you* could not possibly take on people to help you, and that there are some excellent reasons why it's not feasible in *your* business to engage others. I sympathise. Please read on.

When I'm mentoring entrepreneurs, they express three main concerns about taking on help. The first is about money – they ask how they are going to be able to afford to pay people to work in their business. The second is about logistics – they ask how they are going to figure out what the new people will do in the business. The third is about responsibility – they express concern about being responsible for the financial wellbeing of another person.

The first two of these questions are answered in the remaining chapters of the book. The third concern is commendable, but is actually a bit futile – I invite you to get over it.

Forget, for a moment, about all of your concerns. Close your eyes and picture yourself working in your business today. On your own. Doing everything yourself. Working all of your awake hours. If you are going to grow the business, while at the same time doing less work, how will you do it?

Looking at your Current Roles Diagram and comparing it with the Future Roles Diagram, isn't it obvious that some of your current tasks must now be assigned elsewhere? No business is immune from this obvious reality.

Five types of help

Once you have accepted that you need help, the next thing to figure out is what type of assistance it will be.

The help will come from one or more of the following sources:

- Electronic solutions

- Service providers

- Business partners

- Employees

- Trading partners

These five types of assistance are your ticket to greater profitability. And, more importantly, they are your passport to freedom. These solutions will be among your business's most valuable assets. So it's important to select them wisely.

We are going to look at these five types of assistance in the remaining chapters in Part Four.

Keeping freedom in mind

As you start to take on help in your business, remember to keep an eye on the goal, which is to ensure that your working time in the business is steadily and consistently reduced.

Because what we most definitely *don't* want is for your role to switch from producer to manager. In that scenario, while you may have successfully delegated most of your current tasks, you are actually just as busy as you were before.

The reason that you will be just as busy as you were before is that in the role of manager your time will be spent in hand-holding your staff members while they carry out their daily work tasks. Instead of morphing into a manager, we want you to become the freedom entrepreneur.

Parts Five and Six explain how you will remain vigilant against becoming a manager, so that you achieve both personal freedom and rapid business growth.

Starting small

As you read the remaining chapters in this Part, keep in mind that you can choose to start small at every stage.

Where the recommended changes to your business seem too scary to implement all at once, you can take a gradual approach. It's more important that you become comfortable with the process of making the changes, than it is for you to rush too quickly into a massive upheaval which is too disconcerting to sustain.

Once you become used to working with others, and you get used to them doing the stuff that you used to do yourself, you will bask in your newfound freedom, and you will grow keener to delegate more and more of your own work.

Electronic solutions

Most businesses can benefit from electronic solutions. The extent to which you can utilise electronic solutions, or automation, will depend on two things: the type of business that you run, and your mindset.

The first question to ask yourself is what are the tasks that you currently perform that can be undertaken by software or some form of automation.

In most businesses there will be at least a few things that are done that can be performed electronically. The following are examples:

- *Orders* – if your own time is involved in processing customer orders, you could automate the process (or remove a non-automated element). For example, if your business currently takes orders by phone as well as online, you could consider ditching the phone method.

- *Invoicing* – if your business sends invoices, and you currently create each one, you could use software to automatically generate each invoice. This could be tied to your order system and invoices could be sent by email without any intervention by you.

- *Queries* – if your own time is taken up with answering questions from potential customers, add some FAQs to your online presence.

- *Expenses* – software can be used to track, and keep records of, your expenses to save you having to do this manually.

- *Marketing* – many types of software are available that will help you to create and send marketing messages.

Electronic solutions can be very attractive, and using software can lead to a massive increase in productivity and profit. Entrepreneurs who are cautious about taking on people in their business can often feel more comfortable with electronic solutions, for example by utilising software to handle repetitive tasks.

While every business can benefit from using software or online techniques, electronic solutions will never be the complete picture. In other words, your freedom machine will not consist entirely of automated processes. Sooner or later you will also need to create a relationship with real humans.

Service providers

A service provider is a business (or self-employed person) that provides services to other businesses.

Service providers help other businesses to thrive. They do this by taking over the performance of a particular function of your business. Because that function is their speciality, and because they routinely perform similar functions for other businesses, they can usually do it for you better and more cost effectively than you can do it for yourself.

At all stages of the business growth process, service providers can be an excellent source of support. And the service that they provide to your business is often cheaper than taking on staff, especially where the service being performed is not a full time one, or where the provider can give you an electronic solution.

The following are examples:

- You could outsource the answering of calls made to your business number, freeing you up from always needing to be available to answer the phone

- You could engage a service provider to maintain your IT system, so that your own time is not spent in managing the challenges created by any IT breakdowns

- You could engage a researcher or list broker to provide you with the contact details of persons, or other businesses, that may be interested in buying your product or service

- If your business sends out large quantities of mail by post, you could use a mailing company to print the letters, place them in envelopes, add postage, and deliver them to the Post Office

- If you spend time contacting customers regarding unpaid invoices, you could engage a debt collector to do this for you

Alternatively, or additionally, you could take on a virtual personal assistant. This is a person who works for you from a remote location (often abroad). They are usually paid an hourly rate. Virtual assistants could help you to research contacts and potential customers, to handle travel arrangements, to source solutions to specific challenges, to find sellers of products that your business needs or to keep your diary up to date.

As your business grows and you take on staff, you could choose to outsource your payroll function or even to have your whole HR department managed by a business that handles staff salaries via specialist online payroll software.

In short, outsourcing some aspects of what you currently do in your business will free up vital time resources that can be spent on more important tasks, such as pursuing business growth opportunities.

What about paying service providers?

Outsourcing obviously has a financial cost, but the aim is to ensure that the income growth that your business is able to generate by outsourcing some functions will more than pay for the costs of that outsourcing. In other words, the profitability of your business will increase.

And remember that outsourcing aspects of your current work to service providers can be an invaluable part of creating the freedom machine. Engaging service providers is therefore one aspect of the work of the freedom entrepreneur.

How to start outsourcing

Let's consider your business. Ask yourself this question:

What do I currently do myself that it would make more sense for me to outsource?

Make a list of the tasks that can be handled externally. Then choose one of those tasks for your first outsourcing project.

The next step is to find a service provider. There are lots of possibilities. You could do an online search, get some magazines that are published for entrepreneurs and look at the classified advertisements at the back, ask for recommendations from other entrepreneurs or visit start-up business trade shows.

Once you have narrowed your search to a couple of possible service providers, you will want to ensure that they have a good reputation and that they are able to do a good job. Check on-line for testimonials or reviews. And follow-up by contacting the businesses that have used them – entrepreneurs are often keen to pass on their experience, particularly if your business doesn't directly compete with theirs. If there are no reviews, contact the service provider and ask for a list of other businesses that they work for – then contact those businesses to enquire about the reliability and effectiveness of the service provider.

Finally, review the contract terms of your chosen service provider. Many service providers will expect you to agree to their standard terms, and will be unwilling to amend them for you. If you don't like the terms, move along to the next service provider on your list. For complex outsourcing projects that are business critical, you may want to get legal advice on the contractual terms.

That's it. Have fun with your outsourcing project. Start with an easy one. Then move on to outsource more tasks when you become comfortable with the process.

Business partners

Business partners are people who share with you both the burdens and the benefits of business opportunities. Taking on one or more business partners can be an invaluable method of achieving your business goals.

It's common to engage a business partner either at the start-up phase or at a key growth stage. Another excellent time to commence a relationship with a business partner is when you start work on building the freedom machine.

Business partners can be hugely beneficial for the development of your business because:

- They can bring new knowledge and expertise into the business

- They can relieve you from working in one or more aspects of the business

- They will not necessarily expect to be paid anything at the beginning of the relationship

As an example, let's suppose that you have created a business which has a loyal following of customers in your locality or community. You have gained as many customers in your geographic region as possible. Therefore, further growth will only be available if your business can reach further afield.

Taking on a partner who can create and manage the online presence of your business may be the key to expanding your business rapidly, due to being able to reach a wider pool of potential customers. Even better, a new website may incorporate functionality which will electronically manage some of the processes within the business, such as taking orders and creating invoices – freeing up your time to work on expansion plans.

Or perhaps you are technically proficient in creating your product, but you need help in other areas of business management, such as sales and marketing or bookkeeping. A business partner could handle these issues, freeing you up to be able to take the steps that are necessary to grow the business.

In the early stages of business development you may not be able to afford to pay business partners. That does not need to be a problem. Many people are often willing to work for 'free' right now, with the promise of rewards in the future.

Everyone has heard of people who have become very wealthy by working with an entrepreneur in the early stages of a new business – well known examples include people who were 'in at the beginning' in companies like Facebook, Apple and Microsoft. Less famously, there are thousands of people who have benefited from being associated with successful entrepreneurs.

You may be surprised at the extent to which you can obtain the labour of excellent people just by deploying your enthusiasm and passion.

> *"The best way to get someone excited*
> *about an idea is to be excited yourself.*
> *And to show it."*
> – DALE CARNEGIE

Selecting partners

When selecting business partners, it's useful to choose people who share your values. They do not necessarily need to be entre-preneurial in the same way that you are, but they must generally be positive, forward-looking and solution-oriented. And you will need to get along with them – you will be spending a lot of time with these people, so choose ones who you would invite to your home for dinner.

It can be useful to avoid people who have an excessive 'need to be right'. The need to be right is one of the most compelling in the human psyche, and in many ways it is useful – it helps us to crystallise a position which we will promote with great passion, an essential trait for a negotiator or seller.

However, an over-abundance of the need to be right will inevitably be harmful, as it represents inelasticity and lack of open mindedness. Some people are so addicted to the need to be right that they are willing to sabotage aspects of their own lives in order to prove that they are indeed correct about something. Although it can be challenging to spot these people, they are often characterised by a strong preference to work alone and they don't recognise the benefit of hierarchy within an organisation (and therefore are unlikely to be effective at following your rules and procedures). They don't work well with other staff members, since they see team co-operation as a waste of their time.

Your business partners may be similar to you or they may complement you. Although it can be tempting to seek a partner who is just like yourself, someone that is different from you can also be valuable. Your business will certainly benefit from a range of skills and attitudes. Take an honest look at your own shortcomings so that you can hire someone that has attributes that you do not.

You may decide to include someone who has, amongst their other skills, a good eye for detail, and someone who is willing to point out the potential negative consequences of proposals and ideas. It will be useful for you to carefully listen to these alternative points of view since you will not always be right (no one is ever right all of the time).

Although I started my first business on my own, within a short time I was working with three business partners. These people were not paid a salary. Instead, they received a share of the business. Although they worked part-time, having these three partners was invaluable for the business, as they possessed expertise and skills in areas that I didn't. When I went into burnout, they stepped in to run the day-to-day business operations while I was recovering.

For me, a key personality trait for business partners is congruity. Congruity in this context has a specific meaning. A person with congruity is someone who will do what they say they are going to do, by when they say they are going to do it. In other words, it's about reliability. People who regularly find excuses for failing to meet their obligations on time must be avoided. We will delve deeper into congruity in Part Six.

Personal motivation and determination are also important in business partners. The extent to which someone has personal motivation and determination can be gathered by finding out what they have achieved in their life. Examples of accomplishments that require personal motivation and determination include running a marathon, training to climb a mountain, learning a musical instrument or overcoming great adversity.

Handling remuneration

Business partners will of course expect some form of payment or recompense for their efforts.

Ideally the type of remuneration that a business partner receives will be sorted out and agreed in advance of them starting work. It's best to do this in writing, since this will reduce the likelihood of future arguments.

However, the reality is that most entrepreneurs don't think about setting out the remuneration package in writing before taking on someone as a business partner. If you have already taken on partners, perhaps with an unspoken and undesignated 'promise' of future reward, there is no need to panic. But you do now need to have a conversation with your business partners and to set out the position in writing. In some cases, your business partner will be expecting this conversation, and they may get upset if it doesn't seem to be materialising.

One of the main difficulties with not having an agreement about business ownership is that the law will assume that you have set up a 'partnership'. A partnership arises when two or more people work together with common business goals, unless there has been an agreement to the contrary. In the absence of an agreement, there is a presumption in law that the participants own the business jointly, with each partner having an equal share.

Therefore, you need to either set out specifically (in writing) the terms on which people are coming on board with you, or to incorporate your business into a limited company.

The limited company route is usually the best solution since it protects you in a multitude of ways. And each participant in the limited company receives a fixed percentage (with the proportions decided by you) ownership in the business in the form of shares. Although you can use an online agent to form a company for you, it's a good idea to take legal advice on the exact ramifications for you of the limited company's creation.

The great thing about people who help you in the business in return for future reward is that you don't necessarily need to pay them for their work on a weekly or monthly basis, at least at the beginning. There are several options for the remuneration and motivation of business partners, and these are looked at in the remainder of this chapter.

Share of the business

Whether you run the business as a limited company or a partnership, you can choose to give your business partners a share of the business. It is slightly easier to do this with a limited company since the company's ownership will already be divided into a number of 'shares'. You can decide how many shares to award each partner.

For example, there may be 100 shares in the limited company, and you may currently own them all. You may choose to take on an IT expert and to 'pay' them by transferring 5 shares. This will mean that you will need to give 5% of any future profit distribution to the owner of the 5 shares. It also means that your percentage ownership will reduce from 100% to 95%.

A word of caution: offering people a *large* share in the business in return for their work can be exceptionally tempting in the early days, since you will be obtaining people's services seemingly for free. There is nothing wrong with this approach, but take a moment to think about how things will look in a few years, by which time the business could be worth a lot more than it is now.

While you would not begrudge a person who helped you at the beginning from benefitting in the success of the business, would you really want the person to own a large chunk of the business for all time, when they provided you with their expertise for only a limited period during the start-up phase?

Another problem with giving away large chunks of the business in the early years is that it may tie your hands later on. For example, you might want to offer shares to employees or to investors, but you may first need to obtain the consent of the other shareholders.

Think from the future – consider the position from your future successful self. If you are going to give away part of the business, give small percentages (perhaps no more than 5% or 10% per person) and always retain a controlling interest yourself.

Additionally or alternatively, make an agreement with the other business partners that their share of the business will cease (in other words, their share will revert to you or will simply be cancelled) in the circumstance where they stop working in the business. Another alternative is to agree that their share of the business will be purchased at fair (or an agreed) value at the date that the person ceases working in the business. Again, you may need to take legal advice when agreeing these sorts of provisions.

Despite the challenges outlined above, giving people a partial ownership in the business is an excellent way of motivating them, as the value of their holding will grow as the business becomes more profitable. When the business starts to distribute profit, the partners or shareholders will receive part of that payout, providing them with a tangible benefit. The value of their shares will also grow as the business becomes more successful.

Commission

Depending on the role of a business partner, instead of giving them partial ownership in the business it may be more appropriate for you to offer him or her part of the income that directly flows from their activities.

For example, you may be so busy making a product that you have no time to spend on promoting it. Or you may have no experience in, or desire to do, the necessary sales and marketing. Taking on an experienced salesperson and offering them remuneration in the form of commission may be an appropriate step.

Commission is often an excellent solution for the start-up entrepreneur, or at a key growth stage, because it means that money will not need to be paid to the partner unless sales have been achieved.

For extra peace of mind in circumstances where your business sends invoices to customers, you could stipulate that commission will be paid to the business partner only when the payment (on which the commission is based) has been received by the business from the customer. This prevents the need for your business to pay commission on income that has not yet been obtained by the business, and so can help cash flow.

Commission will not be an appropriate solution where the business partner's role within the business in not directly related to achieving sales of your business's products or services.

Payment in kind

Depending on what your business does, it may be that there is some relevant synergy with a possible supplier's business. Instead of paying cash for the supplier's service, your business can provide its goods or services as 'payment'.

For example, suppose you are in the business of carrying out maintenance work on printing machines. One of your customers (a printing company) may be willing to print some marketing brochures for your business in exchange for the work that you do on servicing their machines.

Payment in kind can be an excellent way to obtain services where you do not have spare cash and your business has excess capacity.

Payment with money

Payment with money is the least satisfactory method of remunerating business partners. It involves making payments to them for the services that they provide. Such payments can be made on a variety of bases. For example, you may choose to pay a regular amount of money per calendar month, or you could pay them for each relevant piece of work that they complete.

The disadvantage for the entrepreneur in paying business partners for their work is that there is no sharing of risk. In other words, the business partners will be paid by your business whether or not your business turns out to be successful or whether or not it generates sufficient revenue to cover the additional expense that the partner's payment represents. This means that the business partners will have no direct 'investment' in the success of the business.

If you are considering paying a business partner for their work (as opposed to giving them a share of the profits or a proportion of their sales), think about whether it may be more appropriate to take them on as employee.

Employees

Taking on an employee is an excellent way to delegate your own production work, freeing you up to do more important tasks, namely growing the business and building the freedom machine.

Employees are the workers in your business who receive payment for their time. They can be engaged on a full-time or a part-time basis. Taking on a part-time employee is an affordable way to practise delegation. For example, you could take on a part-time employee to do just one of the jobs that appear in your Current Roles Diagram, while retaining control of the more important things. Once you see that delegation is working well, you can increase the employee's hours and perhaps assign other roles to them.

Taking on an employee for the first time can be daunting. All manner of fears force themselves into your awareness. What if I hire the wrong person? What if I can't get them to do the job properly? How will I afford to pay them?

Breathe deeply. Relax. Thousands of entrepreneurs take on employees. You can too. Remember that you can start small and see how it goes. The first thing I delegated was filling envelopes with brochures and sticking on postage stamps. This task was delegated before we had an office, so an employee came to my apartment on two mornings per week. This was an invaluable learning experience. Part of the hard work that I had done up to that moment was now being done by someone else. Although they worked for only two mornings per week, those two mornings became a very special time.

I was able to do two key things while my new employee was working. First, I could relax for a few minutes. Relaxation, I discovered, is an essential part of creating the freedom machine. Second, I had time to consider business growth – rather than toil in hard work for these two mornings, I was able to use part of that time to think about business development.

Most importantly, by taking on a part-time employee to do a few tasks, I gained the invaluable experience of doing nothing while someone else was working in the business.

Remember that although an employee may not seem to be affordable, the reality of employing someone to do the tasks that you currently do is that you will have more free time with which to grow the business. The objective here is for you to be able to achieve more income than it costs to employ the person. In practice this is usually fairly easy to achieve. By using relevant procedures (Part Five) and delegation (Part Six) you will start to offload your own tasks *in* the business so that you can work *on* the business and thereby morph your role into the freedom entrepreneur.

How do I find an employee?

Unless you know someone who is looking for a job, the first step in finding a suitable person is to advertise the position. Think local coffee shops, noticeboards in serviced office buildings in your neighbourhood, university job centres, or online.

The next step is to choose which of the applicants you will invite for an interview. In order to narrow the list, it is useful to set out a procedure or task that the applicant must do as part of the application process. This will give you an opportunity to weed out from the list those people who do not follow instructions, a vital quality for employees.

You could, for example, ask candidates to submit a 200-word statement on why they think that they are suitable for the job. You may be surprised at the quantity of people who apply for jobs without following the procedure that has been specified – obviously such people will not be suitable for your business.

As far as knowing who the right person is, the best advice I can give you is to ditch the standard methods of assessment. Instead, consider how you *feel* when you first meet the person. Do they make you smile or frown? Do they make you joyous or despairing? Do they hasten attention or impatience? Do you feel that you want to learn more about them, or would you prefer that the meeting end quickly? Intuition is invaluable for determining who will be suitable for your business.

Beyond that, there may be a number of your own factors that you will choose to take into account, as well as some deal breakers. For me, it's important that the person being interviewed has good eye contact and has interests outside of work. Some level of ambition is important too. Watch out for people who seem like they 'already know it all', as these people may not be comfortable following your rules and procedures.

Some employees may be willing to supply you with references that have been pre-written by their previous employers – you may want to check that these types of references are accurate and up-to-date by giving the former employers a call.

You may also decide to give job applicants some kind of test to allow you to assess their suitability for the role. In my business, interviewees complete an 'attention to detail' test, to check their analytical abilities. We present the applicant with a document that contains several deliberate errors, and ask them to locate and correct those errors.

If you already have business partners or other staff members, you will want to know that any prospective employee will get along with the existing team. To test this, you could leave the interviewee alone with team members (without you being present) as part of the selection process. Then ask your staff for their feedback on the person before making a final recruitment decision.

Ensuring that employees do a good job

A significant concern for entrepreneurs who take on an employee for the first time is that the person will not do a good job.

There are two main beliefs that lie at the heart of this unnecessary concern.

The first is that only the business owner can do the job properly. The second is that people will do the bare minimum amount of work that they can get away with, and that they will cut corners and waste resources.

These beliefs are largely incorrect. The reality is that almost everything can be delegated (see Part Six) and that most people want to do a good job.

When employees don't do a great job, it's usually down to one of two causes. The first cause is that they have not been provided with clear information on what their job entails (more about this in Part Five). The second cause is that they have not been given the tools to get the job done. The tools could include a computer, a vehicle, a smartphone, a franking machine, an expense account or anything else that is necessary to do the job efficiently and effectively.

The good news is that you have control over both of these causes. When you provide employees with both the information and the tools needed to do a great job, a great job will usually follow.

Trading partners

Some entrepreneurs achieve business growth and higher profitability by entering into a mutually beneficial relationship with another business.

When selecting another business to be a trading partner for your business, it's important to keep in mind that the goal is for each business to achieve greater profitability due to the relationship. Usually the business that you select will not sell the same products or services as your business.

Here are some examples:

- A restaurant teams up with an independent cinema to offer 'dinner and a film' as a package

- A niche training business hooks up with a training business with a different niche, each advertising the other's training courses

- A home cleaning business agrees that it will use the services of a local dry cleaner for laundering duvets and curtains, while the dry cleaner advertises the home cleaning service to its customers

- A plumbing business regularly recommends the services of an electrician business, and vice versa

- A law firm puts on a conference with an accountancy firm, each inviting their own clients to the joint event at which both firms showcase their services

Although setting up trading relationships takes time and effort, this effort is investment in your freedom and wealth. The anticipated result is that, once the relationship is up and running, your business will achieve a higher level of income without any additional work for you.

A significant advantage of working with a trading partner is that you don't need to pay them anything.

Before entering into a relationship with a trading partner, be careful to ensure that the business you have chosen will not wish to take over your market. For large deals, get legal advice and ensure that a written agreement is in place.

Part Five

How Stuff Gets Done, Even When You are Not There

*"Men occasionally stumble over the truth,
but most of them pick themselves up and
continue on as if nothing had happened."*

– Winston Churchill

The indispensable (and usually ignored) ingredient

When I mentor entrepreneurs, I tell them that getting assistance from others (and giving up hard work) is essential to their success. After they have recovered from the shock which comes from contemplating ditching their control freakery, they express one of two concerns (or both).

The first concern is about how other people will know what to do in the business. This concern is entirely understandable. The entrepreneur has built a business that has taken time to create. It has a lot of moving parts. Only they know exactly how it works.

The second is about how they will ensure that the work actually gets done, especially when they are not around. Remember that the goal is to dramatically increase your freedom time. Freedom means that you will not be constantly present in the business. If you are not there, how can you be sure that your people will do their jobs? It's a legitimate worry.

Part Five of the book addresses these two concerns.

Let's recap where we have got to so far. Assuming that you have been following along and doing the exercises, you now know that creating the freedom machine is the only guaranteed route to escape hard work.

In order to start creating the freedom machine, you have stopped thinking like an employee, and you now think as the freedom entrepreneur (Part Two).

You've investigated how your business actually works, and you have thought about how it needs to work in the near future (Part Three).

You are taking steps to enlist help from others so that you will be freed up to work *on* your business rather than *in* your business (Part Four).

So far so great.

Part Five of the book contains the final piece of the freedom machine jigsaw puzzle. This piece of the puzzle is the most important of them all. It's also the one that is most often overlooked by entrepreneurs.

Overlooking the final piece is a wasted opportunity – partly because ignoring it exposes your business to great risk, and partly because it's the easiest to implement. But although it's the easiest to implement, it is also the most challenging to undertake. It may be the most significant challenge that you have encountered so far.

The reason it's so challenging is because it will seem unimportant to you. Things that don't seem important often get ignored.

Although overlooking the tasks required in this Part is perilous and often terminal to businesses, it's easy to see why it happens. Entrepreneurs get caught up in the excitement of delegating, and in the growth in income and apparent freedom that delegation can bring. They think that they have finally cracked it. Business is on the up, and so is the profit. The heady and exciting times have arrived. It's finally possible to take some time to grab a coffee or even to go out for lunch. The progress is magnificent.

But there is a problem looming.

The problem is that without the final piece of the puzzle, your business can never have a life of its own. Even though you now have some free time, the reality is that the business still depends on you.

To understand this by analogy, imagine your newly structured business as a human being. If you were creating a human being from scratch, you would need to put together a skeleton, and then attach all the additional bits onto the bones – muscles, organs, skin, a circulatory system and all the other stuff. Then what? Just because you put all the parts in their correct places, doesn't mean that it will spring to life. It is still a dead bunch of assembled parts. It can only move around if you attach some strings and take on the role of puppeteer.

Up to this point, you have built the skeleton of the freedom machine. And you have started work on completing its body. It looks, externally at least, to be a properly functioning and effective business. But, just like the human constructed from all the parts, the machine you have built is lifeless. It cannot work on its own.

The lifeless body can be forced to walk around like some animated Frankenstein's monster. But, without relevant internal direction and guidance, it will falter and fail at a major obstacle.

This Part of the book contains the magic ingredient that will give your business the self-direction that it so vitally needs in order to become the completed freedom machine. This magic ingredient will allow you to truly escape, because you will no longer be needed to hold the baby's hand.

The tasks that you will undertake in this Part will result in the business not being dependent on you. This is vitally important, because all the while your business is dependent on you, your hard work will continue. Worse, a business that is dependent on its founder will be chaotic and disorganised. While it is chaotic and disorganised, you cannot expect anyone other than you to properly understand it. And if no one understands it, you will never be free from hard work. It's a circular concept.

Unless you go to work on the final piece of the puzzle, there is no real point in taking on employees and business partners to help you. Because the result, eventually, will be chaos.

So, let's take a look at how to give your freedom machine a life if its own, so that your freedom can begin.

Giving life to your freedom machine

Think about what happens when you take on someone to help you in your business. It could be someone that you have delegated just a few tasks to. Or it could be a full-time employee.

Imagine their first day of work. You greet them at the door. You shake their hand and welcome them to your business. You show them around the office (or your spare room). You point them to their desk. You tell them where the coffee machine is located.

As far as their actual tasks are concerned, you probably already outlined their role in the job advertisement. You may even have given them a written job description. Perhaps you go as far as sitting down with them and talking about the work that they will be doing and what is expected of them.

Finally, you set them off. And you get back to your own tasks.

If you did *all* of that, then well done. Great job. However, it's not enough. It's not enough because you have made two assumptions. These two assumptions are ones that are made by most entrepreneurs.

The first assumption is that the person engaged knows how the business works. The second assumption is that the new person knows and understands the full extent of the job that is being delegated to them.

These assumptions are always incorrect. If you think about it carefully, you will see why they are incorrect.

Just because *you* know the intricacies of how your business works, that doesn't mean that others do. Just because *you* know how to produce whatever it is that your business sells, that doesn't mean that others will. Just because *you* know the best way to respond to a customer complaint in your business, that doesn't mean that it will be handled appropriately by anyone else. Just because *you* know what to do before setting the security system and closing the office for the evening, that doesn't mean that others will have that knowledge.

Even if you have managed to talk about each and every part of their role with the new employee, that's still not enough. It's not enough because they will forget most of what you said. That's human nature. We forget stuff.

The problem is that forgetting stuff will cause failures within the business. Unless, that is, you are around to clear up those failures. But we don't want you to have to be around all of the time. That is not the role, or the lifestyle, of the freedom entrepreneur.

The final piece of the jigsaw puzzle handles all of these issues. The final piece involves creating written business procedures.

Written business procedures are your ultimate keys to freedom because they explain to your people two things. They explain how your business works. And they explain everyone's roles within the business.

Written business procedures therefore constitute the instruction manual that your employees and business partners will use to operate your business. And written business procedures allow you to step away from the constant running of the business, because they take your place.

Written business procedures are the light at the end of a long dark tunnel named hard work.

Why you need written procedures (even though you think you don't)

Here are some characteristics of great businesses:

- They are machines that produce desired results with effortless ease

- They are deliberately made simple to run

- They achieve a reliably consistent result

- They are well ordered

- They train new staff quickly and effectively

- They serve the needs of everyone involved

Each one of these characteristics is best achieved by using written business procedures.

Without written business procedures, on the other hand, it is very difficult to achieve any one of the characteristics. Running a business without written procedures is like going into a boxing match with one arm in a sling and one leg in plaster.

Let's take a look at each of the above characteristics in the context of how written business procedures will achieve the desired results, namely your personal freedom coupled with rapid growth in business profitability.

Procedures de-complicate

A vital ingredient for your personal freedom is that your business is simple to run. This doesn't mean that your business is not intricate. It means that the tasks that constitute the functioning of the business must be clearly set out and easy to implement.

Until the time that you took on help, the disaster-waiting-to-happen remained hidden. But as soon as you take on others in your business, the absence of written procedures shows up like a fish without water.

Even if you verbally instruct your new employee how to do the job that you are delegating, without written procedures you are relying on their recollection to get it right – not everyone has a photographic memory.

Written procedures de-complicate the business by explaining how it works. If your staff members forget any aspect of their job, or they are unsure about how to handle a specific issue that arises, they can refer to the written procedure.

Procedures ensure consistency

A hallmark of a successful business is that it is consistent.

Consistency means that each product or service is delivered in the same way, and with the same level of quality, each and every time. The customer's experience of the business remains constant on each occasion that they make a purchase or make an inquiry.

This is important because it turns out that consistency of experience is a more accurate determinant of business success than the quality of the thing being provided. In other words, as long as the quality is constant, it doesn't necessarily matter that the quality is not high.

Think about your favourite coffee shop or restaurant chain. Why do you keep going back? Is it because they make the best coffee or lunch? Probably not. It's more likely to be because the product meets your expectations, time after time. If you order a double tall latte or a pepperoni pizza, you know exactly what you will get, on each and every occasion, in every location.

Of course, if you provide high quality products consistently, that is wonderful. But if you have to choose between high quality and consistency, then choose consistency. Because consistency will deliver loyal customers – and it's much easier to retain an existing customer than it is to attract a new one.

Loyal customers bring increased sales. Increased sales lead to increased profits. Increased profits open up all the opportunities that you have planned for.

How do you ensure that your business operates consistently without your constant attention?

By using written procedures.

Only by effectively implementing written business procedures can you ensure that your business will provide your customers with the predictability of experience that they are looking for, without you being constantly required to check that it's happening.

Procedures for staff training

When you first take on people in your business, you will most likely train them yourself. But after a while, you will start to delegate the training of staff members – you will either instruct others on how to train your staff, or you will create self-training systems.

Whether you train new staff yourself or you delegate the training, written procedures are your indispensable assistant. Because the time spent training new staff members will be significantly reduced. Training time will be reduced because your people will be referred to the procedure document that goes with their job. They will read the procedures document as part of their training process. For some jobs, this will be all that is needed.

Procedures for answering queries

Your ability to work on building the freedom machine and your capacity to work on growth opportunities are both dependent on you not being constantly needed to handle queries that arise in the business.

Having written procedures means that the time you spend answering questions from staff members will be reduced or removed, since staff members can refer to the relevant procedures document.

Dispensing with the need for your constant presence is good news for everyone. Your people will be delighted that they don't have to contact you every time they have a query. They will enjoy the security that comes with knowing that their procedures manual is close by, and that it will handle most questions that are likely to arise. Your customers will be delighted that answers to their queries will not be delayed until you can be contacted. And you will be delighted that you won't be interrupted when you are on the golf course, or having a lengthy lunch with friends, or skiing in your favourite resort, or reading a book in the garden, or working on your new business plan.

Using procedure documentation as a replacement for your presence is an essential aspect of the functioning of the freedom machine.

Procedures for internal continuity

As the freedom entrepreneur, it's important that you are constantly vigilant against being sucked back into extended bouts of hard work (there is nothing wrong with helping out occasionally – see Part Six).

One event that is a prime culprit for creating this lure is when staff members are absent from work. Although it's inevitable that one of your people will be off sick or be on vacation, a few times per year, you must steel yourself against the temptation of returning to producer work for extended periods. Because you will desperately want to take up the slack by doing the person's job yourself while they are away.

Instead you must do one of two things: either have another staff member perform the essential aspects of the person's job until they return, or engage a temporary worker to get the job done.

In each case, the procedures manual for the person's job (which will be available on their desk) will be all that is needed to enable performance of the relevant role. Any member of staff, or reasonably competent temporary worker, can handle the role simply by reading the procedures document. This leads to less down-time when staff members are absent from work and prevents the need for your own presence.

Procedures for order

Successful businesses are well ordered. A lack of order, on the other hand, leads to inefficiency. Inefficiency means less profitability.

Written procedures give your business the order that it needs by describing the content of the roles within the business. All of your written procedures, taken together, explain how your business functions as a whole.

Procedures for freedom

Most importantly, written business procedures provide freedom for you as the business owner. This freedom allows you the luxury of being able to focus on what's truly important, which is developing entrepreneurial skills, producing business growth and living your life.

Whatever type of business you run, having effective and clear written procedures is absolutely non-negotiable if you want to be a successful business creator.

Written business procedures are the Holy Grail of the freedom entrepreneur.

What is a business procedure?

Think of a business. Any business. Think about how the business actually works.

When you drill down to the basics of what happens, moment by moment, you see that the business is made up of a very large number of individual tasks. Each one of the tasks is a small but vital part of the whole picture.

A business procedure is a set of tasks. And the business, as a whole, is a collection of procedures. It is that simple. And it is in that simplicity that the magic resides.

Let's take a look at a basic business procedure.

Suppose that you feel like drinking some coffee. Perhaps you need to stay awake for some extra hard work. You decide to visit your local coffee shop. Like any business, the coffee shop consists of groups of tasks. Set out below are the tasks that are performed by the employee behind the counter.

The coffee shop

The employee's first task is to greet you and to ask for your order.

His or her second task is to repeat the order back to you, to check its accuracy.

The third task is for your choice of beverage to be communicated to the barista who will be making your drink.

After that comes handling your payment.

The final task is handing over your coffee, and wishing you an excellent day.

Those tasks, taken together, constitute a business procedure. In this case it's a basic procedure for fulfilling customers' coffee orders.

You may be thinking: "that procedure is totally obvious, and therefore it doesn't need to be expressed!" The first part of that thought is correct. The second part is not correct. Please read on.

There are going to be many other business procedures that are used in the coffee shop. Examples include:

- A procedure for opening the coffee shop each morning

- A procedure for cleaning the equipment

- A procedure for preparing the coffee machines, cups, milk and other ingredients

- A procedure for preparing each particular type of beverage – the latte, the Americano, the cappuccino, etc

- A procedure for ordering more supplies when they run low

- A procedure for handling enquires from people asking about employment opportunities

The business of the coffee shop therefore consists of a set of procedures. Each procedure is interdependent with, as opposed to independent of, the other procedures in the business. Each of the tasks within each procedure must be completed in the correct order and at the correct time.

If we look back at the human body analogy, we can see that the body is made up of a large number of procedures. There is a procedure for digestion, a procedure for pumping blood, a procedure for converting oxygen to energy, a procedure for elimination of waste and toxins. Each one must function well in order for the whole system to be healthy. If there is a breakdown in any one procedure, then the person's overall health and wellbeing is adversely affected.

It's like this with your business. All relevant tasks must be completed on time and in the relevant order.

So your work, from now, is to produce a set of written business procedures which describe each of the roles within your business. The set of procedures constitutes instruction manuals for the correct functioning of your business. The instruction manuals are going to be used by your people to operate your business.

Creating written business procedures

Creating written business procedures is relatively simple. It involves downloading knowledge from your head onto paper (or screen). This documented knowledge will constitute the instruction manuals of your business.

The main challenge expressed by busy entrepreneurs is finding the time to write out, or type, the procedures. After all, the work of creating written business procedures is proactive work instead of reactive work. It's important work, not urgent work. Therefore there are countless other things currently vying for your attention.

Nevertheless, the work must be done. Consider it a vital investment in your future.

In other words, you must stop doing the hard work for a while. And you must use the time that is freed up to create written business procedures. Because creating written procedures is the work of the freedom entrepreneur. It's the most important work that there is to be done.

Resistance

At this stage, resistance is very likely to arise. This resistance may take one of a number of different forms or guises – what they all have in common is that they have the effect of dissuading you from doing the work that is needed to produce procedure documentation.

For example, you are probably thinking that this Part of the book can be skipped. After all, *you already know* what your procedures are. As far as others are concerned, surely the way the business works is *obvious,* or at the very least *memorised* by them. And in any case you can verbally explain the tasks to your new or existing staff members if needed.

Surely, therefore, the documenting of procedures is a waste of your vitally precious time.

This type of thinking is resistance in action. And it's always mistaken. No matter what the size or type of your business, or how many people are involved with running it, it is crucial that your procedures are documented.

Unless the procedures are written, your staff will constantly need you for guidance. If they need you for guidance, you will never become the freedom entrepreneur.

So, your resistance to this part of the process of transforming your business into the freedom machine must be overcome. Overcoming resistance is best done by putting everything else to one side and concentrating on the task at hand. Your brain will attempt to find all manner of excuses and reasons why it can't be done at this moment (and all subsequent moments). Don't let this resistance sabotage your aspirations.

So, let's go to work on creating your first written business procedure right now.

Your first documented business procedure

Before we get started on producing the actual document, you must thoroughly understand the relevant aspects of the business tasks that will comprise the procedure that is being documented. After all, it's impossible to document a procedure unless you know what the procedure is.

The good news is that since you are the business owner, you are the one who gets to decide how the business actually works.

Let's imagine that you are currently doing everything in the business yourself. You realise that in order for your business to accelerate its growth (and for you to stop the hard work), you must take on someone to help you. You decide to delegate part of your current workload to a new part-time employee who will be paid an hourly rate. The new employee starts work next week.

It is critical that, before the new person's first working day, the documentation for the person's job is ready. The documentation will contain two sets of information. The first is the basic business information that all staff members need to know. Examples include:

- The names, job titles and contact details of staff and suppliers

- Information on security protocols

- House style for written communications

The second is the stuff that is pertinent only to the relevant role.

So, let's make a start by selecting one role that you intend to delegate.

To document the business procedure for this role, you must watch yourself. This is meant literally. You must watch yourself doing the tasks that you will soon be delegating. Pause after each task to write down what it is that you have just done. The tasks that you describe in the procedure document are the content of the new person's job.

Take care to ensure that the document is capable of being understood by anyone who might read it. After all, the staff member who uses the document may change from time to time. And the future less busy version of you is unlikely to be there to explain what the document means.

Here are some guidelines on producing your business procedure document:

- *Keep it basic* – the business procedure must be an outline of the fundamental steps required for performing the work

- *Make it comprehensive* – all of the tasks that are critical to perform the work are worthy of mention, even those tasks that seem obvious (what's obvious to you may not be obvious to everyone)

- *Use plain language* – avoid jargon that only a select few people would understand. Don't assume any knowledge on the part of the person who will read the document, unless you intend to always employ people who already have that knowledge

The first two of these guidelines seem to contradict each other. But they relate to different aspects of the process.

The first is about the need for written business procedures to be in skeleton form. It is the bare bones of what is required – the essential steps. It is not necessary to describe the meat on those bones. Think of the meat as being your own preferred way to carry out the tasks – that *way* is your own preference, but it is not essential.

The second refers to the requirement that *every* bone in the skeleton must be included in the documentation. Don't miss out any bones when you are creating the business procedure document, otherwise the skeleton will become unstable.

Back to the coffee shop

Let's return to the coffee shop. Here is an example of a business procedure for the role of greeting customers and taking their orders:

Coffee Shop Procedure – Greeting Customers and Taking Orders

1. Greet your customer with a smile.

2. Ask for the customer's order.

3. As each item is spoken by the customer, enter the item in the electronic register.

4. When the customer has finished listing items, repeat the order back to the customer and ask him/her if there is anything else that you can get for them. If the customer wishes to purchase an additional item, return to task 3.

5. When the customer's order is complete, tell the customer the total amount for the transaction.

---

6. Handle the customer's payment in accordance with the "Taking Payment" procedure.

7. For any hot beverage orders, write each separate drink order on a separate sticky ticket and attach it to a clean cup. Pass all cups with sticky tickets to the barista.

8. For all non-beverage items ordered by the customer, place each item in a separate bag and hand the bag/s to the customer.

9. For all cold (bottled) beverage items, hand these to the customer without any additional packaging.

10. Let the customer know to collect the hot beverage/s at the end of the counter, and wish the customer a great day.

There are three things to note about this business procedure (and all business procedures).

The first is that procedures can assume that the person performing the role is already trained in other aspects of the role. In the above procedure, task 3 refers to using the electronic register to input ordered items. The training of new staff members on the use of the electronic register will be the subject of its own procedure document and must precede the person starting work in the role.

The second is that business procedure documents can specifically direct the reader to other procedures – for example, task 6 refers to a separate procedure for taking payments.

The third is that business procedures are a complete overview (skeleton) of the tasks to be undertaken. As such they constitute a stage-by-stage process for the completion of a specific function, or role, within the business.

It's not about micro-management

The purpose of business procedures is not to micro-manage the members of your business team who operate the procedures.

Flexibility must be inherent in all roles. The business procedure is the skeleton, and the flexibility is the meat on the bones.

For example, task 1 in the coffee shop procedure reads: Greet your customer with a smile. Although this task is specific, it allows for the staff member to choose *how* to greet the customer, using words that seem appropriate to the situation. This flexibility is important for this task for three reasons:

1. No one type of greeting will be suitable for all customers – the flexibility allows the staff member to say whatever they feel appropriate in the moment. For example, the way to greet someone who is soaked through due to heavy rain may be different from the way to greet someone who is wearing a swimsuit on a sunny day. Similarly, the way that an employee greets a child might be different from the way that they greet an elderly person.

2. It allows the staff member to perform their tasks within the parameters of their own personal way of behaving. Business procedures must not attempt to turn human beings into robots, all doing and saying exactly the same thing. All of your customers are human beings (even if your client is a corporation, it works via people), and human beings enjoy interacting with other human beings.

3. It allows the staff member to take ownership of the task by allowing them to tailor the way that they carry out the task to suit their own personality. It's important to the success of your business that your staff members enjoy their jobs, and they are more likely to do so if they can be themselves while they are at work.

Although the above comments relate specifically to the task of greeting customers in a coffee shop, the guidelines apply to most tasks. The goal is to achieve flexibility within required parameters.

Business procedures must be task-specific

Take care to ensure that the procedures you create are task-specific, not people-specific. In other words, you are not writing out a job specification for any particular person. You are instead specifying how and when to do the tasks that comprise specific aspects of your business.

This is important because the person who may currently be doing the job will not always be the one undertaking the role in the future (procedure documentation must be future proof).

Business procedures as checklists

Some business procedure documents take the form of a checklist. A checklist is a list of tasks that need to be completed at a particular time.

For example, let's suppose that some of Naomi's customers decide to make their properties available as short-term vacation rentals. In order to handle the additional work that is required by the higher turnover of renters, Naomi takes on a new employee.

The role of the new employee is to make the properties ready for the next guests. The tasks that comprise this role include cleaning and re-stocking the properties. These tasks can be documented in a list format. As each task is completed, the employee will tick off the task on the list.

Since each property may have differing requirements depending on the preferences of the owners, a unique checklist can be produced for each property.

Here is an example of one of Naomi's checklists for a short-term vacation rental property:

Living Room

☐ Clean and vacuum floor

☐ Dust all surfaces

☐ Check drawers – remove any contents left by previous guest

☐ Water plants
☐ Remove trash from waste bin and replace plastic liner

Bedroom

☐ Clean and vacuum floor
☐ Replace bedding
☐ Check wardrobe – remove any contents left by previous guest
☐ Remove trash from waste bin and replace plastic liner
☐ Fluff pillows and cushions and arrange on bed
☐ Place chocolate on pillow

Kitchen

☐ Clean floor
☐ Clean sink
☐ Clean all surfaces
☐ Check cleanliness of cutlery and crockery and wash as needed
☐ Remove trash from waste bin and replace plastic liner
☐ Wash and clean coffee machine
☐ Check contents of fridge and discard anything not needed
☐ Clean fridge as needed
☐ Replace kitchen towel
☐ Top up liquid detergent as needed
☐ Empty dishwasher
☐ Resupply dishwasher tablets if needed
☐ Resupply coffee grounds and filters if needed

Shower Room

☐ Clean floor
☐ Clean toilet
☐ Clean shower area
☐ Clean and polish shower glass
☐ Replace towels
☐ Top up shampoo, conditioner and shower gel as needed

☐ Top up hand soap as needed
☐ Replace toilet roll if required; fold top sheet into triangle

Overall

☐ Check condition of property and report any damage or missing items

Getting started on business procedure creation

So go ahead and create your first written business procedure, even if you don't intend to delegate the tasks within the procedure right away.

Once you have selected a set of tasks that you currently do yourself, take careful notes on each task as you perform them. Once you have completed the list of tasks (a procedure), read it through to ensure that:

1. It covers everything that you did

2. It does not attempt to micro-manage the employee, but allows for flexibility as to precisely how the task is carried out

3. It is clear and understandable

4. It is task specific, not person specific

Once your business procedure document is complete, you could check it by having someone you know attempt to do the job solely by reading the document. It's important that you do not give them any verbal instruction. If they are able to do the job from the document alone, then you have created your first successful written business procedure.

You can now move on to create written business procedures for each aspect of the business that you will be delegating.

Implementing business procedures

After creating your first business procedure document, the next step is communication and training.

In order for your staff members to be able to execute the procedures, they must know what the procedures for their roles are, and they must understand how to use them. In other words, the person who will be performing the role must be informed about the content of the procedure document, and they must be trained in its implementation.

Training staff members in how to use business procedures is not as daunting and time consuming as it sounds. In fact, the better the job you have done in creating the documentation, the less time will be needed for communication and training.

In addition to communication and training, the business procedure documents must be made available for everyone to access, easily and quickly, whenever needed.

And crucially, you must ensure that the procedures are followed every time. In other words, there must be a way to monitor whether the procedures are being used correctly.

Communicating business procedures to staff members

First, decide who will be responsible for communicating the content of the business procedures document to the employee or business partner. For your first procedure document, it's likely to be you. As time moves on, you will be delegating this role to someone else.

Ensure that you, or the person you are delegating the task to, has enough time available to adequately communicate the content of the business procedure document to the person who will be using it.

Let's go back to the example of your new part-time member of staff from the previous chapter.

Think about the set of tasks that you will be delegating to this person. Once you have created their procedures documentation, your job (unless you have delegated it to someone else) is to sit down with the new employee and take him through the business procedure document, one step at a time.

Allow him time and space to read each step in the procedure document. Then check that he has understood the step. The best way to do this is to ask him to explain the step to you. If it becomes clear that he has not understood it, or that he needs further explanation from you, then the relevant step will need to be re-written so as to make it crystal clear. Remember that you may not be there to explain the meaning of the document on the next occasion that it is used.

When you have completed going through the document, and you have explained everything that is not clear, let the employee know that you will make the necessary changes (if any) to the document. Alternatively, ask the employee to make the changes to the document and to send you the new version for checking. In the meantime the employee can use the current version to make a start on his daily tasks.

Communicating the content of the business procedure document is vitally important. It's also an excellent way for you to develop a good relationship with your new staff member. Ensure that the employee gains the impression that going through the business procedure document with him, and his understanding of it, is the most important thing on your agenda that day. Because it is. There is nothing more important to your personal freedom.

When your people understand not only the content of the written business procedures, but also the importance to the business of following the procedures, your freedom is all but guaranteed. Your own role moves from worker within the business to the freedom entrepreneur. Your own time and skills are unleashed to further develop and grow the business. Working on business growth and development is your true calling as business creator.

Making business procedures available

Business procedure documentation must be easily accessible by everyone in the business (unless one or more roles contain descriptions of work processes that you want to be kept confidential from access by other staff members).

It's up to you how you do this. You could print out hard copies and leave them in the office. Or you could make electronic copies available to everyone in the business.

The ready accessibility of procedures is an important step in securing your freedom.

Now, when someone is off sick from work, or on vacation, the description of their role will be available for other team members to access. Someone else in the business will therefore be able to perform the role, or at least the critical aspects of it, until the person returns to work.

When a new member of staff begins work, ensure that they know not only where the business procedures documentation for their own job is located, but also the procedures documentation for all other jobs in the business. And let them know that they will be expected to help out, whenever needed, by performing aspects of other people's jobs.

Checking that business procedures are being implemented properly

It's the old problem. Having a set way of doing things is all very well, but it doesn't work if the set way is not observed.

We have all experienced breakdown in business systems, at least from the perspective of being a customer of *someone else's* business. We are told by an employee of that business, "oh, that shouldn't have happened that way". We might suspect that we are not the only person to have suffered from the issue. And we often think poorly of the business as a result. We might even choose to go elsewhere in future.

We don't want this kind of breakdown to occur in your business.

In order to reap all the benefits of having business procedures in place – consistency in production, speedy and effective staff training, and personal freedom – we must have a way to ensure that the procedures are observed, every time.

Ensuring that business procedures are correctly observed and implemented can best be done in one of two (or both) ways. The first way is to instigate a system of checks.

Who is going to check to see if the business procedures are being implemented correctly and on time? If you said "me", you are partly correct. Initially at least, it will be you. Because one of the roles of the freedom entrepreneur is checking the correct functioning of procedures. But remember that freedom is your ultimate goal. So in the very near future you will be assigning the job of checking procedures implementation to one of your employees.

Checking in this context doesn't mean spying. It's not our goal to 'catch someone out'. On the contrary, we understand that all persons engaged in the business are working cooperatively on the shared goal of excellent customer service and mutual prosperity.

The purpose of checking is to discover whether anything is going wrong and, if so, to take steps to sort out the problem. It's your job, as freedom entrepreneur, to ensure that all staff members understand that this is the goal of checking. Once they become aware of this, they will be happy with the process. Because it supports their goals as well as your own.

The second method of ensuring that jobs are being done properly and on time is one that is self-enforcing. In other words, it doesn't require your ongoing participation. It is done by making procedures interdependent.

Business procedures must be interdependent

How do you get each staff member to *want* to ensure that not only their own job is being done properly, but that all jobs within the business are being done properly?

You do it by making business procedures interdependent.

Interdependency means that the work done by each of your team members is partly dependent on the work that other members of the team are doing. In other words, the job of employee A contains elements that must be actioned before employee B can properly do their job. Rather than being independent of each other, the working roles of A and B are interdependent.

Suppose your business makes candlesticks out of craft cement. The steps that are necessary to build a candlestick might include making the moulds, mixing the ingredients to produce the cement, adding the solution into the moulds, firing the product in a kiln, painting each candlestick by hand and finally placing each candlestick in fancy packaging.

In this example, the person responsible for painting the candlesticks will be unable to do their job until there are candlesticks available to be painted. That's obvious. It is also very useful. Because it means that the job of the painter is dependent on the proper performance of the person who is responsible for mixing and firing the product.

There are several benefits of building interdependency into your business procedures:

- Interdependency encourages internal communication. Where *my* ability to do *my* job properly depends on *you* having done *your* job properly, we automatically have relatedness. Even if we don't work in the same location, we will want to communicate with, and cooperate with, each other.

- Interdependency encourages excellence. After all, most people want to do a great job. Where my ability to do my job excellently is dependent on you doing your job excellently, I will be keen for you to do your job excellently. I may even help you with your job. Or I might make suggestions for improvements to the way that you do your job. The culture within your business will move towards excellence, rather than mediocrity.

- Staff members will want to ensure that their job is 'covered' by others when they anticipate being away from the office or otherwise unavailable. They won't wait for you to appoint appropriate replacement staff. Instead they will most likely handle the situation themselves.

These benefits not only increase the likelihood of great performance among your people, but also mean that your freedom is protected.

Business procedures must be living documents

I want to be clear about something: by insisting that you have documented procedures, I am not advocating a rigid unchanging system for running a business. On the contrary, written business procedures will need to be regularly updated and amended.

After all, changes are inevitable in all aspects of life and business. These changes may be external to your business, or they may be internal. Examples of external changes include these:

- Customers' preferences may alter

- Methods of manufacture may be revised

- New technologies may become available

Examples of internal changes include these:

- One of your staff members lets you know that she has come up with a better way of performing a function of the business

- You realise that the way a person is doing their job is incorrect - when you take a look at the business procedure document, you see that there is an ambiguity that needs to be resolved

- An employee asks you how to deal with a particular situation that has arisen that is not covered in their procedure documentation

Your business procedures documentation must be able to evolve to meet these and other changes that arise. But, here is the key point: existing procedures must always be followed, until they are changed.

Changing business procedures

The first thing to determine is the question of who can make changes to the business procedure documentation.

Will it be only you that can authorise changes to the procedure document? Or will a decision of a senior partner or head of department be sufficient? Or will you decide that the person whose current role is contained in the document can make changes to that document themselves?

If you decide that the person themselves can make the changes, then ensure that the changes are reviewed by someone else before being implemented. The person doing the double checking needs to have a good understanding of the whole business so that she can ensure that the change will not adversely affect the proper functioning of the business.

Once the change has been made, ensure that the change is reflected in the way that your business operates going forward. Update your procedures documentation to reflect the changes. And ensure that your staff members are adequately trained in the new ways of doing things.

Ideally, and especially where changes to procedure documentation will be made frequently, the method for changing procedures will be clearly set out in its own procedure document.

Customer facing changes

If you are making improvements that directly affect your customers' experience of your business or its products, then let your customers know that you are doing it (ideally before the improvements are implemented).

And, once you have made the change, stick to the new way of doing things. Don't waiver back and forth between different ways of treating your customers. They don't like it, and you will be putting your business at risk by doing it.

Your business transformed

So, now you understand the importance of having written business procedures.

Without written business procedures, there is confusion about how the business operates. Where there is confusion, there will be inconsistency in carrying out business tasks. Confusion and inconsistency lead to disgruntled employees and dissatisfied customers.

Documented procedures are not only vital to the survival of your business. They are also essential to your personal freedom.

Once you have implemented written business procedures, your business is radically transformed. It may look and feel like the old business from the outside, but its internal functioning is now very different. In the old model, *you* were the business. After making the changes in Part Five, *the business procedures* become the business.

Employees no longer come to you with a multitude of questions, since they now know where to find the answers. Certainty of job roles produces a happier workforce. Your business now produces consistent results every time, to the delight of your customers.

Your role as entrepreneur moves from working *in* the daily activities of the business to working *on* the development of the business. Your role morphs from producer to leader and delegator. Your time is freed up to expand the business, and to enjoy ever more free time.

Part Six

Your New Role as the Freedom Entrepreneur

"A leader is most effective
when people barely know he exists.
When his work is done, his aim fulfilled,
his troops will feel that they did it themselves."
– LAO TZU

The freedom entrepreneur leads and delegates

As you know, this book is about freedom.

The core message is that unless you have personal freedom, your business is at great risk. Because hard work creates an environment in which you will be unable to function as an effective entrepreneur. The more that you engage in excessive working practices, the less effective you will be. And the more likely that you will go into burnout.

So, your personal freedom is the key to your success.

In order to create more free time for yourself, you must convert your business into the freedom machine. The freedom machine has your freedom as its primary goal.

Once your freedom machine is up and running, the resulting increase in your free time allows you to continue to work *on* your business rather than *in* your business. Working on your business is about taking key decisions, engaging others to work in the business, implementing written business procedures and creating growth opportunities.

Most of the book, up to this point, has been about the steps to take and the mechanisms to put in place in order to build the freedom machine. In other words, it has been about *what* there is to be done.

An equally important question is *how* to go about doing it. Because the manner in which you carry out the work of the freedom entrepreneur is just as crucial to your business success as doing the stuff that needs to get done.

In particular, the way that you handle yourself when you are with your people not only has a bearing on the success of your business, but is the very foundation of that success. Many businesses fail not because they are bad businesses but because the business owners turned out to be ineffective leaders.

Entrepreneurs often express concern that the people they engage in their businesses won't do the things that need to be done. Part Five looked at using procedures to alleviate much of this worry. Part Six goes one stage further – it looks at the behaviour of the business owner. Because whether or not your people do the stuff you want done is not about them – it's about you!

It's about you becoming a great leader and delegator. Being *both* a great leader *and* a great delegator is vital for effective entrepreneurship. Neither one of these two skills is sufficient on its own. You cannot be a good leader without being an effective delegator, and vice versa.

Let's use a made-up word to describe a person who has *both* of these skills in abundance: you must become the 'leadigator'.

> *"Leadership is the art of getting someone else*
> *to do something you want done*
> *because he wants to do it."*
> – DWIGHT EISENHOWER

This final Part of the book therefore looks at key qualities of the leadigator. You can develop and emulate these qualities so that your success is all but guaranteed.

Before getting into that, let's dispel some myths about what it takes to be a good leader and delegator by looking at what the leadigator does *not* do.

The leadigator does not attempt to get her people to do their jobs by instilling fear. Nor does she do it by being cajoling, manipulative, aggressive, belligerent, antagonistic, hostile, deceitful, devious, demeaning, degrading, debasing, domineering, underhanded, wily, tricky, humiliating, shaming, scheming, controlling or conniving.

While some business leaders can 'get away with' these behaviours for a period of time, and even 'successfully' use them to build a profitable business, the reality is that they will eventually lead to poor co-worker morale, poor relationships with customers and suppliers, and, eventually, destruction of the business. Quite apart from that, these ways of behaving might suggest that the business owner is not only insecure, but is actually quite unhappy. Perhaps she is overworked.

What we want instead is for your people to be flexible, loyal, committed, joyful, enthusiastic and eager to do a great job. In short, we want all of your employees and business partners to be delighted that they work in your business.

This Part of the book is about what it takes to be a great leader and a great delegator. Before looking at the key behaviours of the successful leadigator, let's answer an important question: *what is it that you need to delegate?*

The stuff that needs to get delegated

Assuming you have read the entire contents of the book up to this point, you now have a pretty good idea of what must be delegated.

However, we are going to take a look at the question of what needs to be delegated in a slightly different way. We are doing this so that you will avoid a mistake that is often made by entrepreneurs when they are distributing tasks within their expanding businesses. The mistake they make is that they inadvertently increase their own workload as a side-effect of the delegation process.

So, we are going to forget about the distinctions that we've used to categorise types of work up to this point. Just for a couple of pages. We will come back to them later in this chapter.

Instead, we are going to divide the tasks that you will be delegating into three new categories. Here are the three:

- *Category 1 delegation: New work that arises due to business expansion* – this is all the stuff that is completely new. Examples include work that is done to serve the needs of new customers and work that is done on a new type of activity or venture. If you are in the plumbing business, this could be fixing the leaking pipes of the new customers acquired by your business. Or work that arises due to your decision to offer existing customers an opportunity to take out a new insurance plan against costs of future leaks.

- *Category 2 delegation: Work currently done by you that remains static despite business expansion* – this is all the aspects of your own current workload that still need to get done whether or not your business expands. If you run a fitness training business, this could include paying utility bills and rent on the premises, distributing promotional fliers to local coffee shops and maintaining sports equipment.

- *Category 3 delegation: Work currently done by you that increases in quantity due to business expansion* – this is all the stuff that you currently do which will take up more time as a result of business growth. If you are in the insurance brokering business, this could be handling the growing number of queries that arise due to increased marketing efforts.

In order to become the freedom entrepreneur, you must delegate work in *all three* categories. Although many entrepreneurs become adept at delegating work that falls into Category 1, they often forget about Category 2. Even fewer entrepreneurs remember to delegate tasks that fall within Category 3.

To illustrate this, let's take a look at Rob's business.

Rob's business

Rob trained as an accountant. It was what his father had done. When his father retired, Rob agreed to run his father's business, a small accountancy practice.

The practice had a ready-made client list and two part-time members of staff who performed administrative tasks. Rob took over his father's clients and, for a while, things continued much as they had done before.

Because Rob wanted to grow the business, and because there was plenty of work available, Rob decided to take on two additional accountants. Pretty soon each of the new accountants was just as busy as Rob. This was great news, as the business was serving more clients and making more money.

The problem was that although Rob had hoped that he would be less busy after taking on the additional people, the reality was that he was busier than ever.

He was now handling not only all aspects of the work generated by his own set of clients, but also some administrative aspects of the overall larger practice. Although the new accountants were doing great work for the new clients, Rob continued to perform some tasks that related to *all* clients. One of these tasks was completing necessary regulatory paperwork for every client that visited the practice. Another was performing money-laundering and identity searches on all new clients.

Since there were many more clients now than before, Rob was much busier. And he was putting in more working hours with every passing week. Within a few months, the stress of doing all the additional work led to breakdown.

Learning from Rob's experience

Rob did a great job of growing the business. He tripled the number of clients and increased the profitability of his practice.

But when we look at his performance as a delegator, he did less well. Although he took on two employees to handle the additional work that was required to service the needs of all new clients (*Category 1 delegation*), he made two mistakes:

- He failed to use the opportunity presented by taking on help to offload some of his *own* workload (*Category 2 delegation*)

- He failed to ensure that all additional aspects of his own work that arose as a result of business expansion would be handled by others (*Category 3 delegation*)

As a result of these oversights, Rob's workload grew to a much greater level than before he took on help. His freedom time was therefore decreased rather than increased. And the lack of freedom, coupled with his excessive workload, caused burnout.

Always remember that your overriding goal is to increase your own freedom time. Because only in freedom can you become a truly effective entrepreneur. Get used to seeing every change that occurs within the business as an opportunity to build more freedom time into your day.

As you take on each new member of staff, ask yourself the following vital question:

> *How can I use the opportunity presented by this change to give myself more freedom?*

In Rob's case, he could have achieved more freedom by delegating some of his *own* tasks to each new member of staff. But, instead of doing that, he kept his own workload as well as taking on additional responsibilities. Rob's workload therefore increased with each new client acquired by the business.

He had created a ticking time bomb.

What must you delegate?

And so we return to the question posed by this chapter. What do you need to delegate?

The answer, which you hopefully already figured out, is this: *you must delegate everything that is producer work!*

(If you have forgotten what producer work is, take a look at Part Three. And bear in mind that producer work is likely to consist of all three categories of delegable tasks).

If you are not happy with this answer, it's probably because you don't feel comfortable with the idea of delegating almost everything that you currently do. After all, you are a highly successful control freak.

So, let's answer the question in a different way: *for right now, you need to delegate everything that you are comfortable with delegating.*

Initially, the set of tasks that you are comfortably willing to delegate may be small. But, after a short period of time, our aim is for you to become more comfortable with delegating. So comfortable in fact that eventually, and actually quite soon, you will fall in love with delegating. Delegating will become second nature. Delegation will be your best friend. Because delegation is your only route to freedom.

Some things can't be delegated?

At first, you will believe that there are some things that cannot be delegated. I understand. I used to have that same belief.

When I mentor entrepreneurs on delegation, I ask them to produce a list of tasks which they believe that they absolutely cannot delegate. Then we take a look at each task in turn, and we ask the following question:

> *What is the real root of my belief that this task cannot be delegated?*

After we have chatted about it for a while, we usually discover that the underlying reason is either the need for control or the desire for perfection. There is nothing wrong with either of these aspirations, but they will not help you to become the freedom entrepreneur.

So go ahead and make your own list of tasks that you couldn't possibly delegate. Perhaps it is a long list. Perhaps it contains most of the tasks that you currently perform within the business.

Now, pick one of the tasks. Any one will do. For that task, ask yourself this question:

> *If my life depended on it, could I delegate the task?*

Asking yourself the question this way creates a different focus for the problem. Instead of clinging to the perceived impossibility of delegating the task, this way of looking at the issue allows you to see how it might be possible. Providing space for this possibility inevitably leads to consideration of how it *could* be done. This is all that is needed to open your awareness to the prospect of a freer existence. And, in that moment, all your dreams become obtainable.

Where to start

In Part Four, you made a list of your daily tasks, and you divided them into producer work and entrepreneurial work. Take another look at that list.

Everything you have designated as producer work is your immediate target for delegation. Start small. Delegate one item on the list. Then continue to delegate the tasks until you have little, or preferably no, producer work left.

Eventually you will also delegate some of your entrepreneurial work – this will occur naturally once you become adept at the skill of delegation and once you experience the immeasurable benefits that effective delegation will bring.

So now you know *what* to delegate. The final question that the book handles is the issue of *how* to delegate.

The question of how to delegate (and how to lead, which is largely the same thing) is the same as the question of how to *be*. In other words, the key is in your 'beingness'.

Ask yourself how you are behaving when you are with your employees and business partners. Think about the characteristics that you present to them. Because these characteristics will determine whether you will remain successful through the process of business expansion.

For the remainder of the book, the focus switches from thinking and doing to being. So, let's take a look at the 'beingness' traits and skills of the effective leadigator.

Being an effective listener

Effective listening is the cornerstone of great leadership. And it is a vital prerequisite for delegation.

In order to become effective listeners, we need time to listen. Time for listening exists in freedom.

Effective listening, in the context of the freedom entrepreneur, is not just about being silent and allowing other people to have their say. Instead, it has three components: it is active, it is open and it is demonstrated.

Active listening

In order to be an effective listener, you must engage *actively* in the listening.

Engaging actively in the listening requires you to be *available* to hear what is being said. You will not be available if your mind is busy thinking about something other than what is being communicated to you.

There are two requirements for active listening.

The first requirement is a quiet mind. A quiet mind is a fully present mind. Being fully present means that you are completely available in the moment to hear what is being said. A busy mind, on the other hand, is anathema to effective listening. How often do we prevent ourselves from fully participating in a conversation because our mind is elsewhere? How frequently do we detect a silence that arises in a conversation and then have to scroll back in an attempt to recall what the other person said?

The second requirement for active listening is that your attention is fully focused on the person who is speaking. Full focus means that your total awareness is captured by the other person. Full focus allows you to *understand* what the other person is saying *in the context of their reality*. This is important because, in order to truly comprehend the communication, you must put yourself in the shoes of the person who is speaking.

Most entrepreneurs have good intentions when it comes to listening. They want to receive the key messages that they need to hear. And they understand the importance of conveying the impression that they are fully engaged with what's being said.

The problem is that hard work leads to insufficient time for active listening. When we are frazzled and frantic, we are likely to be mentally multi-tasking rather than really listening. In this state, we can only be partially aware of what's being said. Even if we do hear the message, it often leads to a new train of thought rather than to real comprehension.

Active listening, on the other hand, enables you to enter the frame of reference of the person who is talking. Once you are standing in their shoes, you will be in a better position to understand them. Understanding them is the whole purpose of effective listening.

Active listening thwarted

There are two main ways in which we sabotage our own intention to be an active listener. This happens when we are partially-listening and when we are engaged in response preparation.

Partial-listening is when we decide to appoint only part of our awareness to what is being said. We devote the other part of our awareness to another mental activity. Entrepreneurs do this when they feel overly busy or stressed. Their attention may, for example, be on making decisions or handling emergencies, rather than on fully listening.

If we were being less than generous, we could say that partial-listening is more about pretending to listen than about actually listening.

The problem with pretending to listen is that it's always obvious to the other person that their words are not being fully heard. Their communication is 'falling on deaf ears'. This leads to resentment and erosion of respect.

Active listening is also hindered when the listener is busy thinking about a response. In this state, the listener has heard what is being said, up to a point. But their mind is wrenched away from hearing anything further because it is engaged in considering how they will reply.

Response preparation can be very tempting – it saves time later, and it means that your reply is already available when it's your turn to speak. But the problem with response preparation is that you will miss the full content of what is being communicated.

So what can you do if you have thought of a fabulous reply that you want to remember?

Rather than spend time trying to think of a way to recall it later, it's better to make a quick note of the point. If you choose to do this, let the person know that you are doing it ("I'm just making a note of what you are saying") so they appreciate that you are still fully engaged in the conversation.

Open listening

In addition to being active, listening is most effective when it's open.

Open listening requires consideration of what is actually available to hear without allowing what is being said to become unduly coloured by the listener's filters.

A filter in this context is a mental construction that constitutes an 'existing knowledge' about either the person speaking or the subject matter of what is being spoken about. Having filters is an inevitable part of being human, but we need to be able to put them aside so that we can see around the filter to the message beyond it.

For example, you may have come to perceive a particular business partner as 'always complaining'. If you listen to your partner through an 'it's a complaint' filter on every occasion that he or she speaks, you may miss some vital information due to your dismissive attitude towards anything that your partner is saying.

Being able to put aside your filtered listening and actively listen from an open place will mean that you will gain access to information that may currently be hidden from your awareness. It therefore provides you with opportunities that you didn't have previously.

To get past your filters, you must become aware of them. That is all. The awareness will automatically start to dismantle your filters.

So take some time to get to know your filters. Bring to mind each of your people in turn, and see what immediate thoughts you have about them. These thoughts are your filters. Before your next communication with each person, bring the filter to mind, and then just let it go. Letting filters go becomes easier the more you do it. And it will give you access to becoming 'present' in the conversation.

Demonstrating understanding

Being understood is one of a human being's greatest needs.

When your people feel that they are understood by you, their respect for you as their leadigator will grow.

Active and open listening leads to true understanding. But your own true understanding is not enough on its own. Because the person that you are listening to will not necessarily *know* that you have understood.

So you need to go one step further, which is to *show* the person that you have understood.

The best way to show that you have understood is to repeat back to the person what they have said. Of course you are not going to do this for every part of the conversation – that would take up too much time and would be quite annoying. Instead, you will do it for just the key things that are being conveyed to you.

When you repeat back to someone what they have said, be sure to explain what you are doing ("OK, I think what you are telling me is that …"). And make sure to use different words than the words that they used. A parrot can repeat exact words – it doesn't mean that the words have been understood.

By using different words, you will convey your own understanding of what the person has said. If you got it right, the other person will know that they have been both heard *and* understood. If you got it wrong in some way, they can take the opportunity to correct you.

Only when you see that the other person has become aware that they have been understood will it be your turn to communicate. At this stage your own communication will stand a much greater chance of being heard and understood. You get what you give. Listen well, and you, in turn, will be listened to well.

> *"Always listen first. As soon as a person*
> *feels deeply understood, they are*
> *no longer worried about their efforts to*
> *become understood. Then they are able*
> *to come up with solutions that no one*
> *would have imagined initially."*
> – Stephen R Covey

The result of effective listening

Effective listening doesn't merely result in a happier workplace and greater respect for everyone involved.

When you actively and openly listen to your people, you will find that the very act of effective listening produces in them a desire to communicate. This desire can be the source of invaluable information, such as suggestions for ways in which the business can be more successful.

It is your listening that causes this desire to communicate. This is because communication doesn't happen in a vacuum. Messages are transmitted only because there is an intention that someone listens. To put it another way, entrepreneurs who are not good listeners will not be given the opportunity to hear potentially useful information.

Of course, you don't need to implement all of the ideas that are presented to you. But it would be unwise to miss the chance to hear relevant suggestions, some of which you will implement and some of which you won't. Either way, your staff members will be pleased that you have heard what they had to say. And they will be delighted to have been understood.

Remember that the game of freedom entrepreneurialism is one in which the aim is for *everyone* to win. The leadigator must therefore consistently listen for ways in which the business can be improved, to meet the needs of everyone involved. This includes not only your employees and business partners, but also your suppliers and customers.

Finally, being a good listener is not the same thing as being constantly available to listen. In other words, you don't need to be present within your business at all times. Instead, being an effective listener means that you will take the opportunity to listen when you are there.

Being congruent

Being congruent, in the context of the freedom entrepreneur, is about aligning your language with your behaviour. It's about *being* your word.

Being your word is important because it turns out that an entrepreneur's rating for success is dramatically upgraded when what they say they will do is fully aligned with what they actually do.

To put it another way, when your choice of words is always backed up by corresponding action, you are much more likely to succeed in everything that you put your mind to. The reason that you are more likely to succeed is that you have become congruent. Congruency is the foundation for effective deployment of all other entrepreneurial skills.

Matching your words with your actions may sound easy, in theory. But the reality is that it takes extraordinary self-discipline.

For example, suppose that someone you know says that they will meet you in the bar at 7pm, but they actually arrive at 7.30pm. Or suppose that they promise to return a book on the next occasion that they see you, but fail to do so. On one level, these types of behaviour can be called 'normal life' – they are minor misdemeanours that are trivial and inconsequential. But on another level, the level of the successful entrepreneur, this type of behaviour is highly counterproductive and can lead to business failure.

Why is congruity so important for successful entrepreneurialism?

There are three main reasons that congruity is essential for business success.

The first is about self-knowledge or self-image. Think of a person who regularly makes promises that they don't keep. This person will come to know themselves as being unreliable. Such a person has a low personal congruity rating. What this means is that their word has come to mean very little to them. As a result, they may suffer from decreased self-esteem and lack of personal power.

A person with a high level of congruity, on the other hand, usually acts on their word, even when it is uncomfortable or inconvenient to do so. This means that the word of a person with a high level of congruity is as good as the thing it describes – the thing will happen because the person says so. A person of high congruity benefits from an upgraded sense of self-esteem and personal power.

The second benefit of congruity is that a congruent person is seen by others as being reliable. In the context of your business, there is great value in having your people come to know you as a person of your word. They will be more inclined to trust the fact that corresponding results will follow directly from what you say. This kind of reliability is a cherished trait of the leadigator since people are more comfortable following someone who is reliable than someone who is not.

The third benefit of having a high rating for congruity is that your likeability will increase. A person with congruity is better regarded than someone who frequently breaks their promises and obligations. Everyone understands that maintaining congruity takes discipline and commitment – these are traits that are universally admired. Being likeable is a key foundation for people who want others to want to do what is asked of them.

How do you increase your congruity rating?

To increase your level of congruity, you must practise being your word. You must do what you say you will do, even if it's uncomfortable or inconvenient.

For example, if you say to yourself that you will go for a run in the morning, then you must go for the run, even if it is cold and raining when you wake up. If you make a promise to your parents that you will visit them at the weekend, then you must go there, even if a more attractive opportunity arises in the interim. If you say to a member of your staff that you will conduct an appraisal meeting with them at 10am tomorrow, then you must turn up at 10am to conduct that meeting.

The great thing about congruity is that it is *wholly* under *your* control. In other words, whether you are a person of your word is totally up to you. It's your choice, always.

Matching your words and your actions consists of two obvious parts: the things you say, and the things you do. When those two things match, you are in congruity.

Congruity is *not* about honouring anyone else's word. Nor is it about living up to a standard or set of values that has been set by someone else. And it's not about doing the 'right' thing. As such, congruity must not be confused with the separate concepts of morality, legality and honesty. The thing that you do (because you said you would) may well be moral, legal or honest, but then again it may not. An immoral act can be performed with congruity simply by virtue of the fact that you said you would do it.

What if you can't get the thing done?

You can still remain congruent even where you don't do what you said you would do.

However, in order to remain congruent in these circumstances, you must *communicate* the fact that the thing will not be done. The communication, which must be made to everyone who will be affected, must take place *before* the time when the thing was to be performed.

As part of the communication, you must either re-commit to do the thing by a later time or state that the thing will not be done. For example, where it becomes obvious that you will not make the 10am meeting due to being stuck in traffic, give your staff member a call to reschedule the meeting.

Here's the important part: if you didn't let the relevant people know that you were not going to honour your commitment *beforehand*, you must still let them know later. And, leave out the excuses and reasons when you do it. This is where having congruity takes real courage and commitment. Because you must be willing to 'come clean' when you are out of congruity and to take personal responsibility for the situation.

So, let's say that you didn't make the 10am meeting because you needed to take your husband to the hospital. You must get in touch with the employee and handle the situation ("I'm calling to apologise for not showing up at 10am this morning. I'd like to reschedule the meeting for tomorrow at the same time. Can you make that?").

Encouraging congruity in others

Having congruity is a trait that you will most definitely want to foster among your staff and business partners. Because reliability is an essential quality for your people to have, especially since you will not be constantly present in the business.

You can do this by letting your employees and business partners know that you value congruity and telling them what it means to be a person who is highly congruent. And, because your staff will unconsciously emulate your behaviour, always match your own words with corresponding actions.

The result of both you and your staff members conducting themselves with a high level of congruity is that your *business* will have congruity.

Congruent business

A congruent business is not only a highly attractive place to work, it is also loved by its suppliers and customers.

Such a business pays its bills on time. It delivers its products when it says they will be delivered. If one of your people tells a customer that they will call them back within one hour, then that gets done. If your website states that your products come with a 100% money back guarantee, then they actually do. No quibbles. No exceptions.

Imagine a business with high congruity. It is a place where each and every staff member meets their obligations on time. It's a place where things happen when they are supposed to happen. It's a place in which everyone can rely on everyone else. There is clarity and certainty about what everyone is up to. There are no unspoken conspiracies not to do things which are required to be done. Everyone is clear about what everyone's obligations are, and each person lives up to those obligations.

Such a business is a force to be reckoned with. It's unstoppable. It's destined for greatness.

Remember that the ultimate source of the behaviour of your business is you, as leadigator. It all starts with you. It always has done.

The question then is this: will you do what it takes to become congruent?

Acknowledging performance

People crave acknowledgement. Your business partners and employees are no different.

As the founder of your business, you are in a unique position to provide that acknowledgement. It often costs nothing to do, and it can be a great source of happiness and productivity in the workplace. It also means that not only will you be liked and listened to more, but also that your people will be better motivated.

Providing acknowledgements is a vital part of facilitating an environment in which staff members are happy and fulfilled.

What's an acknowledgement?

In the world outside of business, an acknowledgement can be as simple as someone smiling at you in the street. The smile makes you feel good. It's directed at you, and only you. At the very least it's recognition of your existence. It's also a connection between you and another person, if only a brief and fleeting one.

For your business, we are going to look at acknowledgements in a slightly different way. Of course it's great to acknowledge someone's existence, but what we most definitely need to do is to acknowledge *performance*. In this context, performance is anything that is done by your employees or business partners that has one (or both) of two effects.

The first effect is that it promotes the profitability of the business. The second effect is that it contributes to your freedom.

An acknowledgement of performance usually consists of some kind of recognition of a job well done. It doesn't necessarily need to be a financial reward, although it can be. It could be something as simple as a verbal commendation or congratulation. As Dale Carnegie advised in *How to Win Friends and Influence People*, "*Be hearty in your approbation and lavish in your praise.*"

Unfortunately, some business leaders are far too reticent to bestow praise (and much too eager to issue reprimands).

Acknowledgements can be given to individual staff members or to teams within the business. Acknowledgements can include praise, gifts (for example a bottle of champagne or a dinner voucher), enhanced job titles, one-off payments or salary increases. You will need to judge what kind of acknowledgement is appropriate in your business for the various types of performance that you want to encourage. And remember that when several members of staff have contributed to the achievement, the acknowledgement must be given to them all.

Acknowledgements in your absence

Although acknowledgements are essential, they don't necessarily need to be provided by *you*. After all, in your role as freedom entrepreneur you will not always be physically present in the business. Your lack of presence must not be allowed to prevent acknowledgements being made.

Acknowledgements can continue to occur, even when you are not there, by using one (or both) of two methods. The first is to use the technique of game playing. The second is by using visual displays.

Acknowledgements by game playing

Games are not only an excellent way to lighten the mood at work (businesses don't have to be taken too seriously), they are also a fun way to provide acknowledgements. As an added benefit, games can simultaneously be used to further one or more business objectives.

Games can be simple and easy to win. Or they can be complex and take many months, or even years, to fully play out.

A game can be anything you say it is. For example, the object of one game could be to achieve unsolicited positive feedback from 10% of your customers. Another game could be for all participants in the business to become wealthy.

So that the game remains interesting, particularly where the objective of the game will take a lengthy period of time to achieve, there need to be victories along the way. The victories, which are the achievements of your people while playing the game, must not go unnoticed (they must be acknowledged). These achievements could be step increases in production, the acquisition of set numbers of customers, or simply a happy customer. As the leadigator, it's your job to ensure that the victories are acknowledged.

The acknowledgement of a game win (or the attainment of interim goals within a longer game) can be anything you decide. A key aspect of acknowledgements is that it must make the relevant person or people feel good.

Acknowledgements through visual displays

Visual displays represent a low cost and effective method of incorporating acknowledgments into your business without you needing to be present.

A visual display is a graphic representation of the performance of a part of your business. It is a pictorial measurement of how one or more aspects of your business are doing.

For example, suppose that you decide that you want to keep track of the number of sales of a certain product or service that your business achieves each month. The visual display for this aspect of the business could take the form of a graph or chart, with a different colour being used for each of the monthly totals.

For displays to work as acknowledgements, it's important that all relevant staff members can see the results. The best way to do this is to attach displays to common area walls in the workplace.

As an example, one of my businesses publishes professional journals. Every month the quantity of subscribers rises and falls according to how many customers have renewed their subscription, as well as how many customers have taken out a new subscription.

Our office wall display includes a graph for each journal, showing the total number of subscribers for each month. Every month the team have fun calculating the number of subscribers and adding the new total to the wall display. One of the team members uses a coloured pen to fill in a block that represents the new subscriber total. Other staff members watch the process of adding new information to the wall chart, and have even been known to cheer when the number hits a new record.

The Subscription Manager, as well as all other employees in the office, can see the progress of the team's efforts to grow the subscriber base for each journal. The display roots the Subscription Manager's consciousness firmly in a desire to see ever higher graph numbers. And because everyone in the subscription team can see the performance simply by looking at the wall, they are all effectively engaged in subscriber growth.

Similarly, in our training business we ask every delegate who attends one of our courses to complete a feedback form on our performance as a training company. We place customer service and satisfaction at the top of our list of priorities. There is a graph on one of the office walls, which we complete after each course, which shows the percentage of delegates that gave an 'excellent' grading for our customer service. The graph provides a visual gauge of how we are doing in meeting our goal of exceptional customer service and always exceeding customer expectations. And it embeds the need for excellence in the awareness of our team members.

There will be many aspects of your own business that can be measured using visual displays. Examples might include the number of new customers that the business has acquired each week, the total value of employees' commission earned, the growth of the staff bonus pool, the percentage of waste that has been recycled, the amount of money that has been donated to charity, or anything else that is important to you.

The following charts are examples of visual displays:

Monthly Sales Achieved

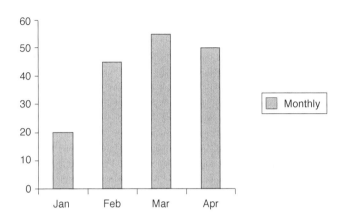

Percentage of Office Waste Recycled (one pie chart per month)

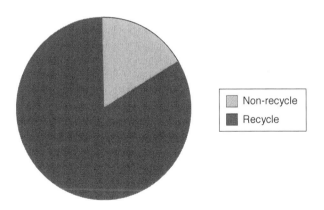

Being one of the team

A leadigator is never 'above' doing work that has been delegated.

She will participate in handling the tasks that comprise all aspects of the business when it is appropriate or expedient for her to do so. In this way, the commander is always ready to demonstrate her willingness to join in the battle, if only for limited periods of time.

In your business, there will be circumstances in which you must be prepared to handle yourself tasks that are normally handled by your people.

In many cases you will have personal experience of the tasks because you did them before you delegated them. But there may be some things that happen within the business that you can't do – that is fine, there is no need for you to be able to do everything.

The circumstances where it will be useful for you to undertake tasks within the business include crunch times when the business is extraordinarily busy and times when the staff member who usually handles the task is temporarily unavailable, such as in the event of a family emergency.

Demonstrating to your people that you are not 'too important' to do the job will have two key effects. The first is that they will respect your willingness to do the jobs that they do and your keenness to help out where needed ("she is one of us").

The second, and the more important, is that your staff members will emulate your behaviour. If you are willing to do someone else's job when that person is unable to do it themselves, your team members will become similarly willing to help out where needed and will even volunteer to stay late to get the job done.

A further advantage of having everyone become willing to help out as needed is that it avoids the human tendency towards demarcation. Demarcation occurs when a staff member identifies with their own role only, and fails to appreciate the benefits associated with helping out other staff members ("I do my job, and only my job"). Demarcation must always be discouraged.

As the leadigator of an effective and well-managed business it will only rarely be necessary for you to help out by doing someone else's job, but taking the occasional opportunity to do it anyway will pay huge dividends.

Being comfortable with uncertainty

Human beings have a need for certainty.

Unless we are students of psychology, we don't need to understand why we have this need. But it's useful to know that it exists and that it tends to show up as a desire for regular employment, a safe living environment and trusted friends – job security, home security and social security.

As entrepreneurs, we must frequently live with much less certainty than non-entrepreneurs. Some business creators find this challenging.

While the freedom entrepreneur has grown to love the idea that we inhabit an uncertain world, and he enjoys the challenge that the unexpected can bring, even he may dread a turn of events that brings about a highly negative situation.

In business, as in life, nothing is certain. In reality, change is the only real constant. And so as leadigators we must develop a level of comfort and calmness around unpleasant surprises.

The more comfortable we are with change, and the uncertainty that it brings, the more effective an entrepreneur we become.

How do you become comfortable with uncertainty?

The first piece of advice is this: don't panic!

When a challenging situation arises, take some deep breaths and know that there is always a solution. Show your people that you are calm under fire. Go for a walk, and take some time to contemplate what has happened, what it actually means (rather than what your greatest fears about it are), and what possible courses of action are now open to you.

You can also practise being comfortable with uncertainty so that you will be better equipped to handle the unexpected when it arises.

To practice being comfortable with uncertainty, you can create insecure situations for yourself to experience. Think of situations that make you uncomfortable, and deliberately seek them out. Or create them.

Here are some examples of things that you could do:

- Next time you ride your bike across a park, close your eyes for a few seconds while pedalling

- Take a new route home from the supermarket

- Call a friend and tell them something you have always wanted to tell them but didn't have the courage to

- Say Hi to the person who sits next to you in the café

- Instead of facing forward in a crowded lift, stand up front and face the back

- Order something different at your favourite restaurant

Each of these experiences is uncertain because you are not in control of what happens. Practising being in insecure situations will develop your ability to handle change, making every new risk (and unexpected occurrences) easier to deal with.

> *"Creativity comes from*
> *the wisdom of uncertainty."*
> – Deepak Chopra

Another way to become more comfortable with uncertainty is to take steps to persuade yourself that you are good at handling surprises. This persuasion can take the form of 'mantras'. A mantra is a statement which you repeat to yourself regularly.

Here are some examples:

- "I can handle any new situation or circumstance that arises"

- "Any unexpected happening, no matter how unpleasant, always carries within it the seed of its solution"

- "There is always an unexpected benefit that arises from difficult situations"

- "I have the ability to calmly and rationally react to new situations"

- "I am comfortable with change"

- "I am an excellent business leader who is highly skilled at making effective decisions"

In essence, to ditch your discomfort with uncertainty, you need to give up being a control freak. You need to acknowledge that the reality is that you can control very little beyond your own behaviour. You need to roll calmly with the Universe despite its many undulations.

This doesn't mean that you can't take steps to steer your business out of trouble where necessary. Your ability to react well under pressure is a key to your success. And you must remain true to your goals as best you can. But you can also relax into insecure situations. And even grow to love the challenges that are sometimes presented by the unexpected.

Being committed to your people

Being committed to your people means that you, as leadigator, conduct yourself in alignment with their interests.

Part of being aligned with their interests is about being committed to their development and growth. It's also about ensuring that they attain job satisfaction and that they are happy in the workplace.

In order to understand how their particular needs will be best served, you will need to listen effectively. And you will need to take steps to implement relevant solutions. For example, one of your employees may dislike an aspect of their job, which you may be able to swap with part of someone else's job. Or a staff member may need some time away from work to handle a personal issue in circumstances when they have no remaining holiday time.

Being committed to your people is also about minding your own behaviour. Because your behaviour will be emulated by your staff and business partners. Where you are honest, loyal and committed to the success of the business, it is much more likely that your people will adopt similar traits. To paraphrase Ghandi, 'be the change that you want to see in [your business]'.

Taking a stand

Being committed to your people also means taking care of them, to have their backs. You must be willing to defend them when appropriate. To be loyal.

For example, customers or suppliers might become dissatisfied or even angry with one of your staff members. Where a grievance escalates into a verbal attack, you will need to take steps to ensure that your staff member is taken care of, even if this means potentially losing a customer. While we have a responsibility and desire to meet our customers' needs, this does not mean that your employees or business partners can be abused.

Sharing success

Being committed to your people is also about sharing the fruits of your business success.

Always remember that the profit that your business generates has been achieved by a team of people. Business creators who hoard all of the benefits themselves will not be successful indefinitely.

The obvious people to include in sharing business success are employees and business partners. But remember too that your suppliers and customers are part of the team that produces the overall result. An occasional gift to these external people will be unexpected, and will generate both gratitude and loyalty.

Being aware

Awareness is essential to successful entrepreneurialism. Because awareness leads to a truer and deeper understanding of reality. The better that we understand the way the world works, the more equipped we are to produce spectacular results.

Frantically busy entrepreneurs are inevitably less aware than those that are calm and composed.

Awareness leads to empathy

Empathy is a vital foundation for the effective deployment of people skills.

To have empathy is to see the world from someone else's perspective. It's to identify with or experience the thoughts, feelings or attitudes of another. Some people call this type of awareness emotional intelligence.

Empathy enables you to understand others from their unique perspective, allowing you to communicate with them on their terms.

Remember that each person experiences the world differently. Every individual has a life path that is unique to them. Each person has a different interpretation for events that occur. No two people see or understand stuff that happens in exactly the same way.

Empathy allows us to understand this. And although having empathy is an essential foundation to effective people handling, the real power lies in what you do with the information.

Let's imagine that you send a message to an employee, asking him to come to your office. The reason for the meeting is to discuss a marketing idea that you came up while you were in the shower this morning. But the employee doesn't know this. From his point of view, there are a multitude of possibilities. And since human speculation tends towards the negative, the employee might think that he has done something wrong. He might even try to figure out what the wrong thing might have been. By the time he gets to your office, he may have worked himself up into an agitated state.

If you engage your empathy, you will be able to tell from the employee's demeanour that he is anxious. And you will be able to use this knowledge to set his mind at rest before you begin the meeting. This will create a space for your communication. Better yet, let the employee know the purpose of the meeting in advance– then he can spend the intervening time being productive instead of worrying.

If, on the other hand, you launch into the meeting without first dealing with the employee's thoughts and feelings, the communication will be considerably less powerful. Because while you're speaking, the employee will be trying to figure out if his suspicions about the purpose of the meeting were correct, rather than effectively listening to you.

How do we become more empathic?

The answer is that we must go to work on our awareness. Awareness in this context means consciousness, and includes being in a state of noticing. To be in this state requires a peaceful and open mind.

In the meantime, if you are unable to ascertain what a person is thinking and feeling then take steps to acquire the knowledge. In the example of the agitated employee coming to your office, you could ask a question that allows him to become conscious of his thoughts. "How are you feeling today?" Or "I'm sure you are wondering why I asked you to come in." This will give you the information that you need to generate a calm space in which the communication can begin.

What must we be aware of?

We must work on raising our level of awareness both generally and specifically.

To be in a heightened *general* state of awareness, or consciousness, is part of our ongoing work in becoming the freedom entrepreneur.

Specifically, in the context of the leadigator, you need to raise your awareness of your staff and business partners. In particular, you need to keep an eye on their strengths and weaknesses, as well as their needs.

If someone is strong in a particular area, for example communicating on the telephone with clients, then allow them to build on that strength by giving them more of that type of work. Where someone is weak in an area, consider whether they need better instruction or training. If they have received appropriate instruction and training, then move them to another area of the business (if the size and structure of your business allows for it). Remember that everyone is good at something, and most people want to do a great job.

Building a strong and sustainable business is about building effective relationships with others – with your business partners, your staff, your external service providers, your suppliers and your customers. Effective relationship building takes awareness.

In order to help develop your awareness in key areas, ask yourself the following questions.

- How are my staff and business partners feeling right now?
  - Is there anything that I can do that may result in them feeling better?

- How do our customers feel when they interact with the business?
  - What changes can I make to the business procedures that will lead to greater satisfaction?

- What do our customers expect from the business?
  - How can we exceed our customers' expectations?

- What do my business partners expect from me right now?
  - How can I both meet and exceed the expectations of my business partners?

- What do my employees expect from me this week?
  - What steps can I take to both meet and exceed those expectations?

Awareness in your team

Once you have gone to work on your own awareness, you need to consider taking steps to raise the level of awareness amongst your employees and business partners. Your goal is to raise the consciousness level of these people in order that the consciousness level of your entire business is increased.

The more awareness that your team members bring to their daily tasks, the more those tasks will produce great results for your business. The more awareness that an employee or business partner brings to their work, the better they will be at meeting the needs of your customers, and of interacting with and assisting each other, and hence of co-creating a better working environment and more profitability.

Ask your employees and business partners questions like these:

- What can we do today to have our customers feel good?

- How can we make it easier for our suppliers to deal with us?

- What strategy can we implement so that our customers will give us an 'excellent' rating in feedback?

Awareness is assisted by greater access to relevant information. So, to increase your awareness, and the awareness of your team members, consider implementing the following:

- Regular meetings with your staff

- Spot checks on the production process

- The gathering of feedback from customers on your products and the performance of your business and your staff members

Being empowering

The book has referred many times to the fact that most entrepreneurs are control freaks and perfectionists. The fact that they are control freaks and perfectionists is perfectly normal.

Your own control freakery and your tendency towards excessive perfectionism are most likely the very traits that led you to your entrepreneurial path. Without such qualities you probably would never have achieved all of your successes thus far.

However, now that you have created your business, you are going to need to reduce your reliance on both of these characteristics so that your business can grow effectively. Because in a growing business it will not be possible, or desirable, for you to have a say in everything that occurs. Instead, we want to foster an environment in which your people will feel able to take decisions without involving you.

Trust your people (don't micro manage)

When you begin to work with others, there will be a temptation to control or micro-manage their behaviour. This must be resisted if you are to be successful in creating the freedom machine.

A sense of personal empowerment amongst your staff members is critical to your personal freedom. And yet allowing your people latitude in how they conduct themselves within the business goes against the grain for the hard working control freak. This means that you must allow your team members to take their own decisions about how their work is undertaken (provided that it remains within the applicable written business procedures).

Remember that the eventual desired outcome (for example, the sale of a product to a customer) is more important than the precise method of getting to the outcome. Your people will feel empowered if you allow them this latitude. Personal empowerment is highly motivating and gratifying.

Consult your people for solutions and ideas

If a staff member asks you what they should do in relation to something that happens, reflect the question back at them. You can ask, "What do you think would be useful to do here?" Increasing their propensity to think for themselves is an essential part of being the effective leadigator. It will also free up your time, since you will not be constantly answering a never ending stream of questions.

Encouraging staff members to think about possible solutions to challenges faced by the business will cause them to understand that you value their opinions. People who feel that their opinions are valued tend to be more empowered than those whose opinions are either ignored or not even sought.

You can also involve your people in the development of new business opportunities or ways of working. Their involvement can take the form of an informal conversation or a more formal meeting. Tell them about your idea and ask them how they think it might work. They will likely come up with proposals for implementing your idea. And they will be able to let you know how the change will affect their jobs.

In pursuing this consultative approach, I have found that staff members have enthusiastically greeted new proposals. They often volunteer to do whatever additional or alternative work is required to bring ideas to life. Sometimes they have pointed out why they think that the idea will not work or isn't appropriate – in a growing business where your staff understand the intricacies of their own roles better than you do, this is invaluable feedback.

Inviting your staff to participate in the creation of new strategies and ideas, as opposed to merely imposing your plans upon them and requiring compliance, will have a profound effect on their alignment with your goals. Their personal sense of inclusion and fulfilment will increase. Because they will have a sense of sharing with you the journey of business development. Of adventuring together into new possibilities.

Embracing mistakes

Human beings dislike making mistakes.

What we dislike even more is the thought of someone else discovering our mistakes. We will do everything we can to cover up our mistake, including lying to ourselves about it.

Many entrepreneurs punish employees who make mistakes by docking pay or refusing promotion. This is the wrong way to handle mistakes.

Our own mistakes

From our own point of view, as entrepreneurs, we usually make mistakes when we are trying something new. In other words, we are less likely to make a mistake when we are doing what is familiar to us, or 'playing it safe'. Entrepreneurialism involves taking risks. It involves venturing into new and untried territory. In that type of environment, mistakes happen frequently. If we are not making mistakes, then we are not playing the game at a high enough level.

Taking on people in your business and delegating work to them will inevitably involve getting some things wrong. That's as it must be. It's the necessary experience of an entrepreneur in a growing business.

A mistake is simply an opportunity to learn. When we ascribe additional meanings to making a mistake ("I am a useless failure"), our willingness to venture into new territory will diminish. When we attempt to hide a mistake, the opportunity to educate ourselves and others disappears.

As an exercise, instead of recoiling from your next mistake, celebrate it! Announce the mistake, and say what you have learned from it. Be joyful in the opportunity to learn. Your partners and staff members will love your easy manner around admitting that you were wrong. And your understanding of the humanness in mistakes will allow your people to feel comfortable enough to reveal their own failures. They will follow your lead by letting you know about their own mistakes rather than spending extensive time and energy covering them up. Your business will be more 'human' and will be a more enjoyable place to work.

Mistakes made by staff members

As I was writing this chapter, one of our newest team members sent a group email to 100 or so external contacts. Instead of putting all the recipient email addresses in the bcc field (as he had been trained to do), he put them in the cc field. He immediately sent me an email saying this: "I want to apologise to you for my mistake – I am aware of the significance of my error and I will not do it again." There was no question in my mind that he would not repeat the mistake in future. That fact makes him today a better employee than he was yesterday. This is a cause for celebration – not only was the mistake beneficial to the future success of the company, but there was nothing to be gained from chastisement.

Start to embrace your own mistakes and those that you see others making. They all enhance our experience and make us more aware. Don't get stuck in the blame game – castigating yourself and others for mistakes – as this is the road to disaster. Why? Because you will be focussing on the negative (life gives you what you focus on). And since you will become known as someone who looks for mistakes in order to ascribe blame, your partners and staff will do their best to hide their mistakes from you.

Remember that mistakes are fabulous opportunities to learn how to do it better.

Final Thoughts

I've suspected for some time that my main purpose on this planet is communication, in one form or another. So when friends and mentees suggested that I write a guide for fellow entrepreneurs, I became intrigued and excited by the prospect.

Although it took the next five years to write it, this book is the product of their suggestion. It is aimed principally at the successful solo entrepreneur, the busy self-employed person and the small business owner. But it may also be useful to an employee who is contemplating starting a business.

If I could make a suggestion, it is that you don't treat anything written in this book as being concrete fact. Instead, the book's content is offered to you as a product of experience. It's a collection of ideas that have worked for me. You can try out the suggestions to see if they work for you. If they do, that's great. If they do not, that's great too. Because each of us has a uniquely valuable experience of business creation.

In my view, the entrepreneur's journey is ultimately one of personal discovery. What is possible in business is limited only by the entrepreneur's perception of what can be achieved. The entrepreneur's perception of what can be achieved is directly related to the extent to which the entrepreneur is able to think clearly – to see things as they truly are.

This quest for clarity and truth, it seems to me, means that business creators are on a spiritual journey. I don't mean this in a religious sense, but rather in the sense of expedition, adventure and discovery. The journey consists of trying things out to see what works; gauging the effectiveness of different courses of action; doing our best to interpret what happens as dispassionately as we can; assisting others to discover their own value and importance; and being a contribution to those we love and to humanity in general.

Once you have arrived at your goal of creating a successful and sustainable business in which your own hard work is no longer required, you may wish to take some moments to consider the magnitude of your achievement.

Against the odds, you have grown your business without excessive work. You have delegated your previous working tasks, thereby creating employment opportunities for others. You have changed the lives of your business partners, your employees, your suppliers and your customers. The world is now a different place than the one that it was at the beginning of your journey.

And so, finally, we come to you in your personal capacity. Now that you have created the freedom machine, what will you do with your newly acquired free time? How will you choose to spend it?

If you don't know in advance what you will do with your new found freedom, then there is a danger that either you will fill it with more work or that you will become bored. Neither of these scenarios is what we want for your life. So I recommend that you take some time to think about your new exciting future. What activities makes you feel most fulfilled in life? Take steps to do what you dream about in your biggest and boldest imaginings.

If you will permit me, I'd like to add a final observation on business growth. After all, much of the material in this book is about growing your business. This is because growth is an essential prerequisite to an entrepreneur's freedom. Without growth, the business creator will not be able to afford to take on business partners and employees to help him. Without others involved in the business, the entrepreneur is consigned to continued hard work, and the chances of him being able to create the freedom machine is close to zero.

However, in my view, 'growth at all costs' is neither an appropriate nor an acceptable goal in the modern world. In fact, putting growth ahead of all other goals has created many of the problems that our planet is currently experiencing, including social, moral, ethical and environmental ones.

Perhaps a better goal is to create a business that excellently serves the needs of its founders and its staff members, customers and suppliers. Going after 'more' may then perhaps be unnecessary. Perhaps a great business is one in which everyone is happy with what the business provides for them. Further growth therefore becomes unnecessary once the goal of contentedness has been achieved.

If this book has touched you in any way, or led you to reconsider any aspect of your role as a business creator, then I am grateful for the opportunity to have made a difference in your life. Perhaps you will one day share your own experience with other entrepreneurs.

In the meantime I wish you an exciting journey into effortlessly successful entrepreneurship.

The author can be contacted at
enquiries@freedomentrepreneurbook.com

68505044R00127

Made in the USA
Charleston, SC
14 March 2017